A highly desirable 2002, freshly restored, is a car many BMW aficionados yearn for. This pretty example has just been professionally refurbished stem to stern for far less than the cost of a new
318i. (Courtesy Peter Fuller, Automotive Import Recycling)

Ken Gross

Illustrated
BMW
BUYER'S
GUIDE

Motorbooks International
Publishers & Wholesalers Inc
Osceola, Wisconsin 54020, USA ®

ACKNOWLEDGMENTS

I'd like to express my sincere thanks to the many people who helped me complete this book. I'm very grateful to Dirk Strassl and Michael Urban of BMW in Munich and especially to Claudia Hoepner who, through persistence in the BMW files, located many of the photographs. I'd also like to acknowledge the support of Halwart Schrader of *Automobil Chronik* in Munich.

Tom McGurn and Tom Knighten of BMW North America were very helpful as were Marc Luckman, Michel Potheau, Bob Roemer, and Yale Rachlin of the BMW Car Club of America, Inc. For the 507 section, Barry McMillan and Albrecht Goertz could not have been more cooperative. Dave Brownell, editor of *Special Interest Autos,* kindly supplied material used in his delightful magazine.

Thanks also go to my editors, Bill Kosfeld and Barbara Harold of Motorbooks International, for believing me when I said I really *was* working on the book—their patience and support are much appreciated.

I'd like to thank my wife, Joan Zielinski, for enduring a lot of lonely weekends while the book took shape. Joan's encouragement made a big difference. Thanks also go to Jeremy Gross, whose support in researching BMW articles and organizing photographs was a great help. And to my good friend Ra, who typed the manuscript: Muchísimos gracias!

First published in 1984 by Motorbooks International Publishers and Wholesalers Inc., PO Box 2, 729 Prospect Avenue, Osceola, WI 54020 USA

© Ken Gross 1984

Printed and bound in the United States of America.
Book design by William F. Kosfeld.

Motorbooks International is a certified trademark, registered with the United States Patent Office.

Motorbooks International books are also available at discounts in bulk quantity for industrial or sales-promotional use. For details write to Sales Manager, Motorbooks International, P.O. Box 2, Osceola, WI 54020

Library of Congress Cataloging in Publication Data

Gross, Ken
  Illustrated BMW buyer's guide.

  1. BMW automobile—History. 2. BMW automobile—Purchasing. I. Title II. Title: Illustrated B.M.W. buyer's guide.
  TL215.B25G76   1985   629.2'222   84-9977
  ISBN 0-87938-165-5 (soft)

Cover photo by Susann Miller.
Car supplied by BMW Excluservice, Rockville, Maryland.

TABLE OF CONTENTS

INTRODUCTION

If ever a company arose phoenix-like from its own ashes, certainly BMW, the famed Bavarian Motor Works, did just that. The firm's exciting early sporting history, its aircraft and motor-cycle heritage, the thrilling prewar Mille Miglia triumphs led by the aerodynamic 328, provide a treasure of folklore for the enthusiast. All this lay buried in the ruins of a once-proud facility. Split in two after World War II, with half of its factory behind the iron curtain, BMW's future looked very grim with regard to any return to fame.

And, when car production actually began again, a series of truly bizarre marketing twists and turns, accompanied by a peculiarly spaced-out product range (imagine hand-built luxury tourers marketed side by side with curious bubble cars) marked BMW's dogged progress forward.

Despite the many near-failures, close calls and wrong turns, a pervasive thread wound through much of the Munich product line. The company always felt that spirited driving should be fun—and it labored to produce cars of quality that lived up to this tenet. As the guidepost in BMW's fabulous museum states: "BMW has always recognized the friendly, emotional connections between human beings and cars, which have long ago brought about the change from vehicle to companion and from car construction to a work of art."

The long, confused BMW trail from the war's end is littered with some fascinating dead ends for the collector. The lovely and graceful 507 convertibles, the ruggedly powerful BMW-Glas V-8 coupes, the lively motorcycle-engined 700's, the exciting 1500 and 1600 sedans that finally pointed the way to today's roadburners—they all offer interesting avenues for the person who wants to drive behind the whirling propeller symbol.

Today, with BMW just a half step in sales behind Mercedes-Benz, and the 535i and the 745i (the fastest sedans in their respective hemispheres), interest in older BMW's has never been higher. As you might imagine, there are cars for every budget, from minicoupes to luxury sedans. If you're interested in acquiring a piece of BMW's splendid history, this book will lead you through the maze of models and help you select the car of your choice.

If you're ready, start by learning everything you can about BMW's—I've listed the best books in the appendix. And don't forget the handy Brooklands roadtest reprints. Join the BMW Car Club of America. It's a growing, active club with many enthusiasts and regional chapters all over the US, and its monthly magazine, the *Roundel,* is one of the most professional club publications in the world.

Searching for used BMW's will take you to many sources. One of the first should be the monthly classified section in the *Roundel.* While these ads are for enthusiasts' cars, with higher-than-average prices, you can bet on a fairly honest description and the fact that the owner can provide a greater amount of information about his or her car than the typical non-involved seller. You'll want to be careful about modified cars in the *Roundel,* however. Many BMW owners are notorious hot rodders—frequently adding performance parts that might improve the car but could detract from its value. We'll talk more about modifications and their impact in a later chapter.

Besides the club magazine, BMW ads can be found in US enthusiast publications such as *Road & Track, Hemmings Motor News, AutoWeek* and *Old Cars Weekly.* The UK's *Autocar, Autosport, Motor, Motor Sport, Motoring News, Classic and Sports Cars* or *Thoroughbred & Classic Cars* are always a good bet too—but watch out for right-hand drive cars here. Germany's *Das Auto Motor und Sport* is another source for the rarer European cars. If that's not enough, you can read France's *l'Auto Journal* and *le Fanatique de l'Automobile,* or Australia's *Wheels.* But don't look at these until you've exhausted the Sunday *New York Times* and Sunday and even weekday editions of major city dailies.

Advertisements are always risky—a seller's description of a car is nearly always more favorable than a buyer's appraisal. But the basic rules of buying any used sports car apply here. If you're not qualified to appraise a car competently, you can (and should) hire a professional to help. An hour or so of a good mechanic's time will tell him (and you) nearly all you need to know about your pending purchase. If the seller resists this type of checking, move on. There are a *lot* of used BMW's out there. The company has sold many, many cars in the US over the years, although, admittedly, some of the more desirable types are in short supply.

There probably aren't a lot of real bargains left—most people know the value of a BMW. But surprisingly, local newspapers and even "Penny Savers" will carry some BMW's at lower than current values. These usually aren't cars owned by your typical BMW enthusiast—and they do bear looking at—but most BMW sellers have a good sense of their cars' worth, and unless the owner needs cash in a hurry, be prepared for some real negotiating.

Can you buy a used BMW today and make a bundle on it? After all, people are fond of quoting the meteoric price rise of the 507 (presently in the mid-five figures) as an example of BMW's value—and for years the company's advertising stressed how little money owners actually "lost" after a few years of ownership.

Truth is, BMW's have held their value well, until recently, because the strength of the mark versus the dollar and a growing appreciation here for German cars made it easy for manufacturers to steadily increase their prices—pulling up and inflating the values of the older models in the process.

Here's a case in point. If you have a 2002 like many enthusiasts who began their BMW love affair with this model, the relatively expensive current base model might well be out of reach for you. Still, you can take your 02 (or purchase one in good shape for $3500-4500) and

BMW's dramatic headquarters looks like four cylinders on posts. The imposing structure was completed in early 1973. (BMW Werkfoto)

BMW's come by their handling reputation honestly. Besides this factory test track in northeastern Munich, there's a computer test bed that simulates the famed Nürburgring—and there's always the autobahn. (BMW Werkfoto)

by doing your own restoration and improvements, you'll have a delightful, sporty performer at less than half the cost of the newer (and still slower) model.

If you're not particularly handy, but the reconditioning concept sounds appealing, firms like Air Automotive of Allentown, Pennsylvania, will take your car and completely remanufacture it—updating and modifying shocks, tires, wheels; adding air conditioning etc, if you wish.

For many BMW diehards, the move from the 2-Series to the 3-Series—characterized by a gradually more refined car with slower performance for bigger bucks—was the beginning of the end. The controversy between the 2002 aficionados and the 320i advocates still fills the *Roundel*'s letters column, much like the intense Ford versus Chevy rivalry in *Hot Rod Magazine* in the sixties.

BMW's European models were quite different from the cars sold in the US. Unlike many manufacturers, BMW persisted in overlapping some of its series, and adapting to the ever-changing DOT regulations on an as-needed basis. Before you import a European car, make certain you're aware of the emissions and safety standards for its year of manufacture— or you may find yourself in the midst of expensive conversion work to satisfy the DOT, EPA and other agencies.

Additionally, BMW's maze of models, especially in the early days, occurred because the company was truly searching out the correct marketing direction, and many models, although they were made in small quantities, persisted (like the early 501/2 Angels) for years. In a given year, BMW often made improvements and changes on a running basis—and as these improvements were made, owners sometimes retro-fitted them. Solex carburetors were replaced by Webers, stock shocks gave way to Konis and Bilsteins, carbureted 2002's became 2002tii's.

Most people feel this is fine, as long as the car remains a BMW; others decry the practice and insist on strict originality. The BMW Owners Club Concours rules allow separate classes for stock and modified Bimmers. By the way, "Bimmer" is the popular nickname for a BMW car and "Beemer" or "Beastie" are the affectionate names for BMW motorcycles— don't ask me why!

Once you've made your decision, and you're certain of the make and year BMW you want, and you've made the important decision as to whether your new car will be a show car or a daily driver, you'll need to decide who will work on it. Some of the early BMW's are relatively simple, and comparatively experienced people, backed by a comprehensive manual, can do most of the work in their own garages.

All but the most enthusiastic BMW dealers will neither be interested in nor will they in all likelihood have the parts for a pre-1965 car. Don't despair. Use the BMW suppliers who advertise in the *Roundel* as a parts source and find a good imported-car mechanic. If he knows his trade, and understands your concern for the car, you'll reach a common ground. And don't worry if his name isn't Klaus or Fritz; the Vignali brothers have always taken good care of my BMW!

It's appropriate here to talk about the basics of what to look for in purchasing a well-used BMW. Let's use the 2002 as an example, as that model will undoubtedly be a popular collector choice in the years to come: The 02's are unit-bodied cars and, despite factory and dealer efforts at rustproofing, the body shells can and do rust. If you're looking in the West, this might not be a problem; but if the Bimmer of your dreams has just been unearthed in Vermont, beware: Carefully inspect the front fenders and look for rust along the door pillars and around the directional lights. Also check the joint between the fenders and the front bumper apron.

Other cancer sources are the bottom of the doors (where the inner and outer panels are married), the spare wheel well in the trunk and the underside rear edge of the trunk. Traditionally, BMW's haven't suffered from wheel arch deterioration, and the quality of the early factory paint was quite acceptable.

BMW expert Michel Potheau pointed out that 1975 and 1976 cars are subject to serious rust under the carpet on the driver's side. This can (and does) occur on cars which would otherwise appear to be in concours condition.

After you've decided the body passes muster and any dents or missing parts are fixable, have a look at the MacPherson struts. If the top rubber mount is bad, you can readily spot it. If the shocks are sagging, new inserts are available. Be sure to closely examine the condition of the ball joints and the bush at the front of the lower tension strut. BMW's excellent worm-and-roller steering should be checked for play (any slop can usually be eliminated by adjusting the steering box). With the car up on a lift, you can also examine the ball joints in the steering linkage, peruse for any leakage from the rear shocks and ensure that the rubber boots around the halfshaft universals are flexible and not torn or split.

BMW engines, if maintained, will last and last. Remember, they were designed to take hour after hour of flat-out autobahn cruising. Two things to look for, though, are signs of oil leaks from the crankshaft front seal (a spray of oil along the underside is the clue here) and exhaust smoke on overrun (a hint that valve guide replacement is in order).

BMW's single-overhead-cam arrangement is a good design, but years of high-revving miles will take their toll on the heads, rockers and rocker shafts. Signs of this malady include high oil consumption, noisy valve gear and difficulty in adjusting to the proper clearances.

The 2002 tii Kugelfischer fuel injection has its gremlins, too. If defective, this excellent mechanical system, replaced by Bosch electronic on the later 3-Series cars, will be hard to start, surge at idle, use copious amounts of fuel and diesel on after the ignition is switched off. (Take care here as parts for this setup are becoming hard to get.) This is particularly true on six-cylinder cars where the number 1 and number 2 valve eccentrics often wear beyond maximum adjustment and result in damage to the crankshaft. It's also a concern since the car, besides being down on power, won't pass emissions testing in any jurisdiction.

BMW's rugged gearbox should soldier on nearly forever, although you should look for imprecise shifting (probably worn bushes in the gear selector) as a clue to the car's condition. Similarly, drive shaft troubles are rare, but be sure to inspect the front rubber coupling (the one that goes to the gearbox) and the rubber center bearing. Check to ensure the differential has fluid and if it needs changing.

Exhaust system checks are easy. Plenty of aftermarket headers and mufflers are available, so if the pipes are shot, you'll be able to locate replacements.

Test the brakes while driving the car and inspect the rotors for rust, which indicates the car hasn't been driven much recently. Brakes should have a firm pedal, no pull to the side and no tendency to lock.

Cosmetically, a careful look at the car's exterior and interior (don't omit the trunk, either) will say a lot for how the owner maintained it. Look for BMW inspection stickers, see if the last lubrication record matches the mileage on the odometer. Be sure to check lights, wipers, heater, air conditioning, radio, and so on. All of these cost time and money to repair if they're inoperative.

When you're through inspecting, and if you're satisfied by your test drive, be sure to keep a careful record of work and parts needed so you can bargain with the seller to remove the estimated cost of these items from the price. Once you've done that, then you can negotiate in earnest! If you can, compare your intended purchase side by side with another BMW of the same year and make—by now, you've probably made a lot of friends in the BMW club who'd be glad to help.

Before we get to individual models, here are a few general thoughts on the purchase of an older BMW. The very early cars are nice collector pieces, but they're unsuited for daily driving. Parts are a problem, sheet metal is unobtainable for starters, but more importantly, the early 500-Series cars lack the brakes and acceleration needed in today's demanding traffic conditions. This is also true of the charming but odd (and very slow) Isettas and 700's.

If an early Bimmer is your choice, plan on a later car for regular use. On the other hand, the 1600's and 2002's with a bit of restoration (and upgrading if you choose) are the equal of many modern sports sedans, at a much lower price. You'll have a distinctive little classic that will bring you a great deal of pleasure and admiration.

If you yearn for a 507 but find the price out of reach, take comfort in the fact that the six-cylinder coupes of the early seventies are affordable, perform relatively close to their expensive new counterparts, and are still contemporary in road feel and styling.

There's a wide range of choice in postwar BMW's. Come on along while we learn the players, separate the knaves and discover the gems!

Most BMW restorers can't resist a few improvements. This 2002 has a Weber carburetor and a low-restriction air cleaner. (Courtesy Peter Fuller, Automotive Import Recycling)

This nicely restored 2002 represents great value, has contemporary performance and can readily be maintained. No wonder 02 aficionados love 'em. (Courtesy Peter Fuller, Automotive Import Recycling)

INVESTMENT RATING

★★★★★ The best. Top prices, top value and highest likelihood of continued appreciation. These cars probably won't be advertised in newspapers or magazines. Most of the cars in this elite group are sold like rare antiques: occasionally at auction, but most likely between knowledgeable collectors. Prices are in the low- to middle-five figures, and increasing.

★★★★ Nearly the best. Cars in this category are more affordable than the top cars, but they're still relatively expensive and are often traded from one enthusiast to another. Ads for these cars will appear in enthusiast publications. Prices are steadily rising for these gems.

★★★ Excellent value. These BMW's combine collectability with affordable driveability. They're readily available and, while considered desirable, they are most certainly practical classics.

★★ A nice car, built in great numbers, or a comparatively rare but uninteresting BMW. These cars aren't likely to appreciate much. But they are Bimmers—often of historical interest from one of the company's many transitional periods.

★ It's still a BMW, but it's probably a wreck or a substantially nonoriginal car. One star is really a condition rating, not a class criterion.

Reading between the lines, the comparatively few custom BMW convertibles, or those cars built in limited production, like the 1600 convertibles, are worth an additional half star. Deduct one-half to one star for heavily modified cars in any category.

CHAPTER 1
500, 501, 502, 3.2

501	1952-54	★★★
501A	1954-55	★★
501/6	1955-58	★★
502/2.6	1954-61	★★
501/8	1955-61	★★
502/3.2	1955-61	★★
502/3.2S	1957-61	★★
2600	1961-62	★★
2600L	1961-64	★★
3200L	1961-62	★★
3200S	1961-63	★★

BMW's 500 Series began some of the seeming contradictions that would move the Munich firm ahead, in zigs and zags, through the postwar years. When manufacturing restarted in Munich, the Bavarian Motor Works (formerly a heavily-bombed Luftwaffe engine plant) resumed active work by stamping out kitchen pots from coal-scuttle helmets and even fabricated metal cabinets in a brave effort to regain its prewar status.

The road to recovery began with a 500 cc motorcycle, the R24, which met with a warm reception in a ruined Germany where most people had precious little money for transportation. Yet, as soon as BMW could resume car production, it began with a high-speed limousine, despite the fact that the war-torn economy, supply shortages and strict speed limits seemed to doom the effort from the start.

There was method to this seeming madness. Although a mass production car would have made marketing sense, BMW had no funds for the high tooling expenditure; it needed a car that could be built largely by hand. Competition from the company's former subsidiary in Eisenach, East Germany, almost scuttled the relaunch. The Easterners, with Russian backing, had a year's headstart and sold their Model 340, a warmed-over prewar 327 with a garishly redesigned front end, to a number of car-hungry European countries.

The first new BMW 501 was presented at the 1951 International Automobile-Ausstellung, with a price tag of 15,000DM—about fifty times the average worker's monthly wage in those difficult days. Neatly splitting British and American powerplant ranges, the Müncheners began with 1,000 prewar two-liter 326 engine castings, but an experimental alloy V-8, designed by Alfred Bohning, was already under development.

Actual production of the new cars hinged perilously on supplies. Pinin Farina had first crack at a redesign but his proposal was rejected because it bore too close a resemblance to an Alfa Romeo. Updated Model 335 bodies from coachbuilder Baur of Stuttgart became the specification and after several fits and starts, serious volume production began in October 1952, with the first deliveries taking place in December.

The 65 bhp 501 initially came only in black. While deceptively fast-looking, it lacked the power (remedied in later years) to be a real autobahn cruiser. The car was nicknamed Baroque Angel and while not competitive in early sporting trials, it was loved by taxi drivers who could depend upon high engine mileage with low fuel use.

As sales caught on, refinements began to improve the car. A dual-downdraft Solex carburetor appeared, followed by 12-volt electrics and a separately-located, column-shifted ZF gearbox. Also, a lot of effort went into updating aerodynamics and vision.

The 501 hit a stone wall at 85 mph so the first order of business was a carburetor and camshaft update (for 72 bhp) in March 1954. This model, called 501/A/B, is to be avoided as

A postwar baby Bimmer, the tiny 513 prototype, with its 600 cc motorcycle engine, was a 1949-50 experiment that never reached fruition. Although the sales volume of a little car might have been welcome, BMW, unable to fund the tooling costs, elected to build bigger cars largely by hand. (BMW Werkfoto)

501/501A/501B	
Engine	
Type:	in-line. water-cooled 6
Bore x Stroke (mm):	66x96
Displacement (cc):	1971
Valve Operation:	ohv
Compression Ratio:	6.8:1. later 7.0:1
Carburetion:	one Solex 30 PAAJ
BHP (mfr DIN):	65@4400/72@4400
Chassis and Drivetrain	
Transmission:	4-speed manual
Steering:	bevel gear
Front Suspension:	double A-arms. torsion bars
Rear Suspension:	solid axle. torsion bars
Axle Ratio:	4.255
General	
Wheelbase (mm/in):	2835/111.6
Track front/rear (mm/in):	1322/1408-52.0/55.4
Brakes:	drum/drum
Wheels/Tires:	16x4E/5.50x16
Units Produced: 1.706 (1952-53). 2.251 (1954-55). 1.371 (1954-55)	
Maximum speed (kph/mph):	135/84. 140/87

Notes: The 501 was essentially based upon BMW's prewar 326. Early 501 bodies were built by Baur until BMW production facilities were ready. The 501B was the simplified. lower-priced version.

501/3	
Engine	
Type:	in-line. water-cooled 6
Bore x Stroke (mm):	68x96
Displacement (cc):	2077
Valve Operation:	ohv
Compression Ratio:	7.0:1
Carburetion:	one Solex 32 PAJTA
BHP (mfr DIN):	72@4500
Chassis and Drivetrain	
Transmission:	4-speed manual
Steering:	bevel gear
Front Suspension:	double A-arms. torsion bars
Rear Suspension:	solid axle. torsion bars
Axle Ratio:	4.225 std. 4.551 optional
General	
Wheelbase (mm/in):	2835/111.6
Track front/rear (mm/in):	1322/1408-52.0/55.4
Brakes:	drum/drum
Wheels/Tires:	16x4E or 15x4½K/5.60-16 or 6.40x15
Units Produced:	4.645 (1955-58)
Maximum speed (kph/mph):	145/90

Notes: The 501/3 had the 501's engine bored out 2 mm. Sechs-zylinder BMW's were built simultaneously with the V-8's. Coupes and cabriolets from Autenrieth and Baur were also available.

problems with the new valvetrain saw BMW paying out a great deal of money in guarantee work and the payoff was only an additional 5 mph.

The answer for speed and prestige came in the 2.6-liter alloy V-8 which bowed as the 502 in July 1954 and developed 95 bhp. The basic engine persisted, with only a few changes until August 1961. It was a precedent-setter as Germany's (and the world's) first high-volume alloy V-8. Neat features included five main bearings, a heat exchanger built into the block, a nearly square bore-to-stroke relationship and an honest 100 mph in top gear.

The 502 was distinguished by a V-8 badge on the molded trunk lid and a distinctive whistle at speed which soon became the hallmark of a BMW. By September 1955, the 502 had a wraparound rear window, driving lights and lusher trim—accounting for a nearly 1,500DM price increase. Bargain hunters could buy a V-8-powered 501 for about 14,000DM.

Sales steadily increased to a high of 4,500 units in 1955. BMW was very aggressive that year with the launch of the sporty 503, the stillborn but elegant 505 and the magnificent 507. The basic sedan, which probably paled a little in comparison with its elegant sisters at the Frankfurt show, saw its share of improvements. The V-8 engine was now 3.2 liters but the company, supposedly losing 4,000DM's on each car, and dangerously overextended with the new sports models, was near collapse.

Rival Mercedes was outselling BMW by five to one but the company stood firm, turning down merger proposals from American Motors, the Rootes Group and even offers from the Bavarian state government. Money-saving design rationalizations appeared in late 1957: The 501 got the 02's bigger rear window (less the chrome trim) and engine choices for the range included a 2.1 liter six, the 2.6 V-8 and two speed queens, a 120 bhp V-8 and a 140 bhp luxus 502S. The Mercedes 220S sold for a lot less money, emphasizing Daimler-Benz' smarter choice of a volume market for its cars. By 1960, only 661 big Bimmers found buyers and, despite a slight upturn during the following two years, BMW struggled through the launch of the 1500 (the car that would save the company) and had little money left for improvements to the aging beam-axle Angels.

The 3.2 Super with a 112 mph top end was still the fastest German car (although historian Jerry Sloniger said that, popularly, Germans wished for this "silky BMW V-8" in the lovely new Mercedes body). BMW aficionados had to make do with disc brakes instead of a facelift, and BMW further confused matters with a bewildering profusion of model designations for what was still basically the old 502.

As 1960 rolled around, the S-types featured twin carburetors, servo-assisted brakes, up-rated tires and Benz-beating performance. The old, round motorcycle taillights were deep-sixed the following year; the 2.6 Luxus was now called the 2600L; the 3200L had the former 140 bhp S engine; and the 3200S featured a 160 bhp rating that urged the seemingly ageless Angel to 120 mph. The big sedans finally disappeared in March 1964 with sales limping along at a few hundred units. Fortunately, the 1500's sales were on the rise and BMW had to drop the old four-doors to make room for increased production. Still, the Bavarian government, which hated (as Sloniger pointed out) the idea of having to use Prussian (northern West Germany) cars, petitioned the Müncheners right till the end to save the Angels.

Very few of the 501-Series cars made it to the US and sales of the 502 variants were never high in the US. Full convertible 500's by coachbuilders Baur and Autenrieth were limited production cars (see the section on rare BMW's) available through the factory on special order. These are the crown jewels of the Baroque Angel series. As a historical note, the optional sunroof on the V-8 sedan was one of the first such uses of this now-common feature.

If you manage to locate a clean example of a 500, be prepared for parts availability problems. Try to pick a car that has disc brakes, and drive it slowly to BMW club functions. If you're in love with BMW history, you might wish to own an Angel. If not, put your restoration efforts into one of the sportier, later variants.

The 502 had a number of distinguishing features: a chrome strip marking the beltline, built-in fog lights and the V-8 emblem on the trunk. The second-series 502 had an enlarged rear window. (Courtesy Yale Rachlin)

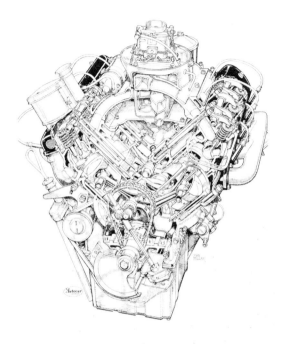

The 502's aluminum engine was Germany's first postwar V-8. The power that would make the legend was about to make itself felt on the autobahn. (*Autocar* drawing courtesy BMW Munich)

502/501 V-8

Engine
Type:.......................... aluminum water-cooled V-8
Bore x Stroke (mm): 74x75
Displacement (cc):.................................. 2580
Valve Operation:...................................... ohv
Compression Ratio:................................ 7.0:1
Carburetion: one Solex 30 PAAJ, one Zenith 32 NDIX (1957-61)
BHP (mfr DIN): .... 95@4800 (501), 100@4800 (V-8, 502)
Chassis and Drivetrain
Transmission:.......................... 4-speed manual
Steering: .... bevel gear
Front Suspension: .... double A-arms, torsion bars
Rear Suspension:.................. solid axle, torsion bars
Axle Ratio:.. 4.255
General
Wheelbase (mm/in): 2835/111.6
Track front/rear (mm/in): 1330/1416-52.4/55.7
Brakes:....................... drum/drum: 1960-61, disc/drum
Wheels/Tires:..................... 15x4½K/6.40S-15L
Units Produced: 5,955 (1954-61)
Maximum speed (kph/mph):........................160/99
Notes: BMW's first V-8 car, Germany's first postwar V-8 car, early 502's are distinguished by extra chrome trim and foglights mounted in the lower front fenders. In September 1955, a wraparound rear window was standardized. The 501 V-8 (April 1955) was the low-buck version, sans some trim and the big rear window.

---

502 3.2/502 3.2 Super

Engine
Type:.......................... aluminum water-cooled V-8
Bore x Stroke (mm): 82x75
Displacement (cc):.................................. 3168
Valve Operation:...................................... ohv
Compression Ratio:.................... 7.2:1, 7.3:1 (Super)
Carburetion: .... one Zenith 32 NDIX
BHP (mfr DIN): .... 120@4800, 140@4800 (Super)
Chassis and Drivetrain
Transmission:.......................... 4-speed manual
Steering: .... bevel gear (power assist optional in 1960)
Front Suspension: .... double A-arms, torsion bars
Rear Suspension:.................. solid axle, torsion bars
Axle Ratio:................................ 3.89 or 3.90
General
Wheelbase (mm/in): 2835/111.6
Track front/rear (mm/in):............. 1330/1416-52.4/55.7
Brakes:................ drum/drum or optional disc/drum
Wheels/Tires:... 15x4½K/6.40S-15L, 6.50/6.70H-15L (Super)
Units Produced: 2,582 (1955-61), 1,158 (1957-61)
Maximum speed (kph/mph): ...... 170/105, 178/110 (Super)
Notes: The 3.2 Super had front disc brakes standard after October 1959. The big BMW's gave off a unique whistle at high speeds that became a distinctive signal to clear the lane on the autobahn.

The 3.2's 6 mm overbore yielded 120 bhp. The 3.2 Super had front disc brakes standard by October 1959. Wide whites add a sparkling touch to this elegant limousine. (BMW Werkfoto courtesy Richard O. Neville)

2600/2600L

Engine
Type:.........................aluminum water-cooled V-8
Bore x Stroke (mm): 74x75
Displacement (cc): 2580
Valve Operation: .... ohv
Compression Ratio: 7.5:1
Carburetion: .... one Zenith 32 NDIX. one Zenith 36 NDIX (L)
BHP (mfr DIN): .... 100@4800. 110@4900 (L)

Chassis and Drivetrain
Transmission:......................... 4-speed manual
Steering: .... bevel gear
Front Suspension: .... double A-arms. torsion bars
Rear Suspension:..................solid axle. torsion bars
Axle Ratio:.. 4.255

General
Wheelbase (mm/in): 2835/111.6
Track front/rear (mm/in): 1330/1446-52.4/56.7
Brakes:..................................... disc/drum
Wheels/Tires: 15x4½K/6.40S-15L
Units Produced: .... 1.639 (1961-63). unknown for L
Maximum speed (kph/mph): .... 162/101. 166/103 (L)
Notes: Disc brakes became standard equipment on these cars in 1961. Taillights were reduced in size and painted to match the body color.

3200L/3200S

Engine
Type:.........................aluminum water-cooled V-8
Bore x Stroke (mm): 82x75
Displacement (cc): 3168
Valve Operation: .... ohv
Compression Ratio: 9:1
Carburetion: .... one Zenith 36 NDIX. twin Zenith (S)
BHP (mfr DIN): .... 140@5400. 160@5600 (S)

Chassis and Drivetrain
Transmission:......................... 4-speed manual
Steering: .... bevel gear
Front Suspension: .... double A-arms. torsion bars
Rear Suspension:..................solid axle. torsion bars
Axle Ratio:.. 3.90

General
Wheelbase (mm/in): 2835/111.6
Track front/rear (mm/in): 1330/1416-52.4/56.7
Brakes:..................................... disc/drum
Wheels/Tires: .... 15x4½K/6.40S-15L. 6.50/6.70H-15L (S)
Units Produced: .... 416. 1.027 (S) 1961-63
Maximum speed (kph/mph): .... 175/109. 190/118 (S)
Notes: In its day. the 3200S was the fastest German production car and accelerated from 0-60 in 13.5 seconds.

The 3200 was the last of the 500-Series derivatives. Its variations included the 2600, 2600L, 3200L and the 3200S. The S-type's 160 bhp V-8 and 118 mph top speed made it the fastest German production car of the day. (BMW Werkfoto)

The 501/3 was built from 1955 to 1958 with a slightly overbored (plus 2 mm) six. Regal Angel could top 90 mph. (Courtesy Halwart Schrader)

Sumptuous 3.2 interior had armrests on both sides for rear passengers. Wraparound rear window introduced in September 1955 represented an evolutionary updating of a rather dated shell. (BMW Werkfoto courtesy Halwart Schrader)

503 1956-59 ★ ★ ★
505 1956-57

The 503, which preceded the lovely 507, shared something in common with BMW's traditional sedans, and with its sportier new sister: the chassis. Count Albrecht Goertz' first work for BMW began with a 502 chassis. The resulting 413 coupes and cabriolets, called 503's, were built over a four-year span. While lovely GT cars in many ways, they were much too big and clunky to be considered sporting models.

The now-famous Frankfurt show, in September 1955, found two traditional rivals in marked contrast. While Daimler-Benz exhibited its W196 Grand Prix car and the Mille Miglia-winning 300SLR, BMW's redesigned 500 Series was a styling step forward.

Starting with the 502's frame, Goertz fabricated an elegant 2+2 in hardtop and convertible models. Some weight was saved using BMW's alloy, 140 bhp 3.2 V-8, as well as aluminum hood and trunk panels. The basic body was steel.

As luxury tourers, the big 503 was positioned against the 300S Mercedes and could even have been considered a bargain rival for the elegant Bentley Continental.

Series I 503's retained the 502's drum brakes and unsporting column shift. Later Series II cars were updated with front disc brakes and a floor shift. The remote-mounted four-speed gearbox ensured a lot of room for front-seat passengers, who could relax in deep leather recliners.

Creature comforts abounded; electric windows and widely-mounted fog lamps were part of the specifications. Coupe purchasers could also opt for a sunroof.

With the powerful twin-carb V-8 up front to move nearly 3,300 pounds, the factory claimed a 118 mph top speed. The long hood and deck allowed a design that approached prewar classic proportions. BMW's twin kidneys were executed vertically and the motif was continued in two contrasting horizontal grilles.

The price tag, for closed or open versions, was a colossal 29,000DM. This tariff was 12,000DM more than the dowdy, but not all that dissimilar, 502.

503's are understandably rare today and the usual, early-BMW caveats apply. High marks for rarity are offset by scarce spare parts and the high cost of restoration and maintenance. Still, the sheer elegance of BMW's first postwar luxury tourer has its devotees.

BMW's really interesting aberration of 1955—the 505 limousine—is a car that had Mercedes written all over it. Of course, the fanfare for the 503 and the 507 relegated the new limo to the background. And, if it hadn't, most likely the price alone would have scared everyone away.

Was BMW targeting this extended-wheelbase (119.5 inches) sedan at Rolls and Bentley? Was the car to be a revival of the custom sedan tradition, to be sold in chassis form only? Historians differ on the rationale but it's undeniable that this lavish limousine, with its electric divider rear window, intercom system, heavy use of wood trim and so on was certainly positioned for the top of the market.

Sadly, orders failed to materialize. The show car was used by Chancellor Konrad Adenauer and then returned to the factory, where it remains on display in BMW's fabulous museum.

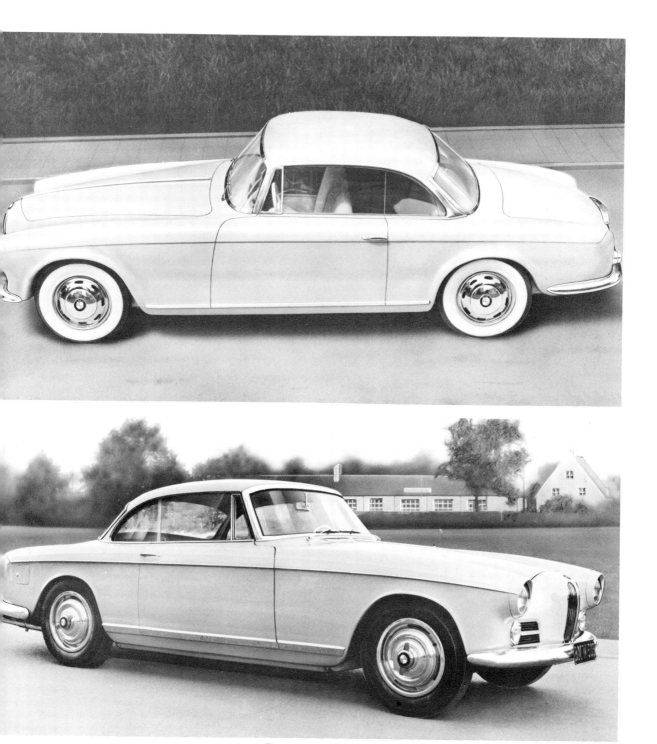

Two views of the elegant 503 coupe. These were big cars and, even with alloy bodies, they weighed more than BMW's contemporary sedans. Knock-off wheels were an extra-cost option. The basic wheel and slotted hubcap were standard equipment. (Courtesy Halwart Schrader)

Interestingly, later Mercedes 300 sedans, particularly the roofline and rear window contours, bore more than a casual resemblance to the ill-fated 505. Surely BMW's only post-war limousine entry was the subject of much discussion in Stuttgart; it remains a fascinating dead end in Munich's history.

A smart design from any angle, the Goertz-designed 503 cabriolet was an elegant statement for BMW. (BMW Werkfoto)

Elegant steering wheel and big gauges made it simple for 503 drivers to navigate. Thin spokes evoked sports-racing-car practice but the over-all effect was pure opulence. (BMW Werkfoto courtesy Halwart Schrader)

The 503 cabriolet's simple but effective rear styling set off a subdued but very commanding presence. Lack of "jewelry" allowed beauty of the curved surfaces to show. Heavily-padded top carried on a German tradition. (BMW Werkfoto courtesy Halwart Schrader)

The elegant 505 Pullman limousine was styled by Giovanni Michelotti. Only two cars were built. The greenhouse and rear fenderlines had a strong Mercedes resemblance. (BMW Werkfoto)

505 interior combined many styling touches of the period: wraparound windshield; big, baroque steering wheel; and the beginnings of a modern dash arrangement. (BMW Werkfoto)

503	
Engine	
Type:	aluminum water-cooled V-8
Bore x Stroke (mm):	82x75
Displacement (cc):	3168
Valve Operation:	ohv
Compression Ratio:	7.3:1
Carburetion:	twin Zenith 32 NDIX
BHP (mfr DIN):	140@4800
Chassis and Drivetrain	
Transmission:	4-speed manual
Steering:	spiral bevel gear
Front Suspension:	unequal-length A-arms, torsion bars
Rear Suspension:	solid axle, torsion bars
Axle Ratio:	3.90 (optional 3.42)
General	
Wheelbase (mm/in):	2835/111.6
Track front/rear (mm/in):	1400/1420-55.1/56.9
Brakes:	drum/drum
Wheels/Tires:	16x4½E/6.00H-16
Units Produced:	412 (1956-59)
Maximum speed (kph/mph):	190/118

Notes: Coupes and convertibles were available. Early cars had remote gearboxes and column shifts. After September 1957, the gearbox was moved behind the engine facilitating a floor shift. All 503 bodies are light alloy but lavish trim kept weight similar to the 3.2 sedans.

CHAPTER 3
3200CS
1962-1965

The last gasp of the BMW luxury V-8—and a forerunner of the later 6-Series sports coupes—was the 3200CS. It was introduced, along with the 1500 model, at the 1961 Frankfurt show.

This new car, which would total 603 units produced slowly over a four-year span, used the 3200S sedan mechanicals as a starting point. The CS retained the big, 160 bhp V-8 but, in a dramatic move to lend some Italian styling grace to the boxy Teutonic design, Nuccio Bertone was called upon to lay out and build a pretty, four-place coupe body.

The bare steel shells were built in Turin and shipped to Munich for trim and final assembly. These coupes were nearly as heavy (4,100 pounds) as their sedan counterparts, but reasonable aerodynamics permitted a 124 mph top speed. At 29,850DM, the price topped Munich's all-time charts.

By the time the final 3200CS coupe (one convertible was specially built for Harald Quandt) was assembled, BMW's direction had shifted and the company changed course to volume-build the new, small 1500 Series. These fast-moving, even faster-selling sports sedans provided the funds for BMW to return to the luxury tourer wars with the 2000C coupe in 1965.

Bertone BMW's retained the distinctive BMW frontal pose. The rear roofline and an angled-back window accented with the BMW badge hinted of cars to come. Again, as a distinct rarity, the 3200CS is becoming of more interest to collectors, but its sporty successors are the coupes to keep.

3200CS

Engine
Type:	aluminum water-cooled V-8
Bore x Stroke (mm):	82x75
Displacement (cc):	3168
Valve Operation:	ohv
Compression Ratio:	9:1
Carburetion:	twin Zenith 36 NDIX
BHP (mfr DIN):	160@5600

Chassis and Drivetrain
Transmission:	4-speed manual
Steering:	spiral bevel gear
Front Suspension:	unequal-length A-Arms, torsion bars
Rear Suspension:	solid axle, torsion bars
Axle Ratio:	3.90 (3.70 optional)

General
Wheelbase (mm/in):	2835/111.6
Track front/rear (mm/in):	1330/1416-52.4/55.7
Brakes:	disc/drum
Wheels/Tires:	15x5J/6.00H-15L or 185 HR 15
Units Produced:	603 (1962-65) Note: some sources say 538
Maximum speed (kph/mph):	200/124

Notes: The 3200CS body was a Bertone design. The Bertone badge appears on the front fenders. A convertible prototype was built but never put into production.

Still using the long, sedan V-8 chassis, the 3200CS succeeded the 503 coupe after a three-year lapse. The smart Bertone body set a standard for future BMW sport coupes with its economy of line, attention to detail and simple, yet positive, styling features. (BMW Werkfoto)

Bertone 3200CS convertible prototype was a one-off; management at BMW declined to approve it for production. (Courtesy Halwart Schrader)

3200CS dash and steering wheel are period pieces—thin wheel, big dials are substantial— similar to those of the 507. (BMW Werkfoto courtesy Halwart Schrader).

Viewed from the rear, the 3200CS short deck, restrained lighting and trim subtly understated its elegance. These cars are beginning to find favor with collectors. Their 124 mph top speed adds to the appeal. (BMW Werkfoto)

Side elevation underscored Bertone's skill in making a relatively large car look purposeful, even graceful. With only 603 3200CS's produced, this rare BMW is worth restoring. (BMW Werkfoto courtesy Richard O. Neville)

CHAPTER 4
507
1956-1959

For BMW aficionados—and those who simply love collector cars—there's a standout from Munich that commands top dollar. Besides one special prototype, with a unique body design, the factory only built 254 Type 507's, so the most outstanding BMW design is also one of the rarest. It's safe to say, because each 507 was virtually hand-built and running changes were incorporated during the model's brief life span, that all the 507's were "prototypes."

This low-slung roadster's timeless grace makes the car look contemporary today, nearly thirty years after Count Albrecht Goertz sketched its classic lines. The slim silhouette, pinched waist, gently arched fenders over tall tires and dramatically raked windscreen all spell speed. The 507's 3.2 liter V-8 packed a lot of punch for its time—when it was properly tuned.

The 507 made its debut at the 1955 Paris show. Remember, the only really exotic cars of the time were the Ferraris and the 300SL Mercedes. At a much lower *planned* price, BMW appeared to have cleverly hit its marketing niche.

Sadly, the 507 only lasted two and one-half years. BMW built the sportsters alongside its prosaic (and overpriced) 503 sedans and convertibles. The factory longed for a sports car to recapture the glory of the fabulous prewar 328, so it persisted in building the 507 beyond any sense of practicality. With low volume the culprit, the actual price tag was *double* that of a Jaguar XK 150.

It's reliably said that Munich lost money on every 507. While popular in its early days in Europe, the 507 wasn't frequently seen in the US. BMW, under Max Hoffman's able direction, as yet had no really effective overseas dealer network. Moreover, the car's nearly $9,000 price tag (the 300SL was available for $8,000) separated tire-kickers from would-be owners quite effectively.

The 507 had some other problems, too. It overheated in traffic and ran too cool at high speeds. The unique in-block oil cooler wasn't effective. Carburetor floats had the nasty habit of overfilling while idling, and on hot days underhood fires sometimes resulted. Parts for the alloy engine were always hard to come by.

Nevertheless, the 507's smashing design elements—rakish two-seater body; torsion-bar suspension; finned Alfin brakes; and aluminum ohv V-8 connected to a crisp, four-speed gearbox—were all sports car. Handling, with stock Koni shocks and the relatively sticky Continental Extra Super Rekords, was quite acceptable. Tall, 3.70 gearing allowed 125 mph autobahn speeds. An optional 3.42 ratio, coupled with a highly tuned 160 bhp engine, was reportedly good for 140 mph—hardly a boulevard cruiser.

Collector interest in the 507 began slowly, but as BMW became more popular in the seventies and eighties, collectors remembered the lovely convertibles and eagerly sought them out.

According to BMW authority Barry McMillan, many cars remain with their original owners. In fact, some people who sold their 507's years ago bought them back. Now, a 507's rare appearance on the market causes quite a stir. When the Henry Ford Museum sold its model late in 1983 for $45,000 (and the car was resold for $54,000 six months later), it simply confirmed what car enthusiasts have known for a long time.

A remarkable design triumph, Albrecht Goertz' BMW 507 was flawless from any view; a car that still looks contemporary. During the photo session for this 507 owned by Norman Wolgin, curious spectators thought the car was a new BMW (Alan Weitz photo courtesy *Special-Interest Autos*)

The 507 was a stylist's triumph. Count Goertz went on to design the 240Z Datsun. Known as "the quiet classic," the 507 is a true star, valued in the Mercedes 300SL range, so be prepared to write a sizeable check. Barry McMillan estimates that there are about seventy-five cars in the US. Three 507's are known to have been destroyed, so that leaves quite a few to look for!

If you are fortunate enough to locate a 507, many engine components are interchangeable with its sister series, the 503. Among collectors, the optional hardtop is highly desirable as are 507's with Rudge knock-off disc wheels, disc brakes (available toward the end of the series) and the very rare metal tonneau cover.

Rust won't trouble you—the bodies are all alloy—but as the lovely sheet metal was formed by hand, no two cars are exactly alike and replacement coachwork will have to be custom crafted. The Zenith carburetors are common to early Porsches. A discreetly hidden electric fuel pump will cure the flooding malady, nicely. It's probably safe to say that a 507 in *any* condition is worth restoring.

Watch out for hotrods. With scarce engine parts a problem, some people dropped Chevy V-8's into 507's. The result was an alarming acceleration rate and a corresponding decrease in the car's value. If you find one of these hybrids, hold on to it and look for an original engine.

Worried about value retention, some enthusiasts have asked if BMW would ever build a limited-production, special-bodied convertible roadster again. That's "highly unlikely" according to a top-ranking factory spokesman, although there's talk of a 630-based convertible for 1985-86. In any case, modern Mercedes convertibles have scarcely affected pricing of the 300-Series classics. One thing you can be certain of, the graceful 507 will remain the definitive BMW styling triumph, and the most significant of Munich's early postwar production.

507

Engine

Type: . . . . aluminum water-cooled V-8
Bore x Stroke (mm): 82x75
Displacement (cc): 3168
Valve Operation: . . . . ohv
Compression Ratio: 7.8:1
Carburetion: . . . . twin Zenith 32 NDIX
BHP (mfr DIN): . . . . 150@5000 (some sources claim 160@5600)

Chassis and Drivetrain

Transmission: . . . . .4-speed manual
Steering: . . . . spiral bevel gear
Front Suspension: . . . . . unequal-length A-arms, torsion bars, antiroll bar
Rear Suspension: . . . . solid axle, torsion bars
Axle Ratio: . . . . .3.70 (optional 3.42, 3.90)

General

Wheelbase (mm/in): 2480/97.6
Track front/rear (mm/in): 1445/1425-56.9/56.1
Brakes front/rear: (1956-57) drum/drum. (1958-59) disc/drum
Wheels/Tires: 16x4½E/6.00H-16
Units Produced: 253 (1956-59)
Maximum speed (kph/mph): . . . . . . .200/124 (with 3.42 gearing 220/137)
Notes: With the 507's shortened wheelbase. (2480 mm vs 2835 mm) the gearbox was attached to the engine and a front sway bar was added. All 507 bodies were alloy. The hardtop was an extra-cost option.

Big steering wheel is a period piece, yet comfortable today. Large, easy-to-read instruments are a plus. (Alan Weitz photo courtesy *Special-Interest Autos*)

The 507 cockpit was snug but roomy. Space behind the seats held soft luggage. Clean door handle design was in keeping with the car's theme. Engine vent was functional. (Alan Weitz photo courtesy *Special-Interest Autos*)

Contemporary shot features a hardtop-equipped 507 in a lovely alpine setting. The standard wheels are shown. Rudge knock-off hubs were an option at extra cost. (BMW Werkfoto)

Convertible top was simple to erect and folded flat for installation of the optional hardtop. Fenderline sculpting softly accentuated the car's flowing lines. (Alan Weitz photo courtesy *Special-Interest Autos*)

Side view showed optional starburst hubcaps. Designer Goertz preferred the slotted wheels. Disc brakes were available near the end of the production run. (BMW Werkfoto)

Clean, purposeful rear was helped by guardless bumpers and beautifully curved trunk definition. (Alan Weitz photo courtesy *Special-Interest Autos*)

Aluminum V-8 was good for 155 bhp, more in specially tuned racing versions. Four-speed gearbox was standard, with two optional rear end ratios. (Alan Weitz photo courtesy *Special-Interest Autos*)

CHAPTER 5
Isetta, 600
1955-1962

Depending upon your point of view, inclusion of the little Isetta in a BMW buyer's guide is either an outright transgression or, more appropriately, a not-too-subtle reminder that, were it not for this funny bubble car, the quick, responsive BMW's everyone admires today might not have emerged.

Back when this funny egg was hatched, BMW suffered from an extreme marketing dichotomy: selling expensive cars in an era when most Germans were still recovering from World War II. In 1955, BMW's new models, the elegant 503 and exquisite 507, attracted longing stares but little else from a German public eager for affordable wheels.

In the meantime, Renzo Rivolta, (a refrigerator manufacturer, who later built the exciting Iso sports cars using his car royalties) designed a practical scooter car in Italy that provided an attainable answer to the prevalent mass transportation question. Trouble was, you had to take the Milanese Isetta on its own terms—and they were quite unusual.

Combining a box-section frame, tubular cross-members and a bastardized Dubonnet independent front suspension, Rivolta built a minicar that was four inches shorter than a VW and weighed half as much. BMW desperately needed an econobox. Rivolta's design was for sale. The addition of a proven BMW motorcycle single (with a whopping 13 bhp squeezed from its 295 cc engine) gave the newly hatched egg some reliability, and the Suez crisis came along just in time for panic-stricken people to appreciate the Isetta's steady 45-50 mpg capability—not to mention its out-of-breath top speed of nearly 60 mph.

While a number of companies built Isettas under license, BMW's total, nearly 160,000, topped the list. Most of these cars have self-destructed, so rolling up to a BMW function in one of the survivors guarantees an appreciative smile. No serious Bimmer collector should be without one.

As if styling weren't enough, Isetta aficionados have to contend with the single door that opens in the front, a backward H-pattern shift and a narrowed three-wheeler-like rear end. Of course, if you accept just one of these little inconveniences, you've only yourself to blame. (Incidentally, while a few three-wheeled Isettas were built, most cars actually had four wheels, with the rear twin wheels mounted close together.)

Originally, the BMW Isetta sold for 2,850DM in Germany. It was $1,100 in the US, well below a comparable Volkswagen.

The Isetta started in April 1955 with a 247 cc version and went to 297 cc. Then, in December 1957, a 582 cc 19.7 bhp twin (adapted from the R60 BMW motorcycle) was offered, on a stretched chassis with a single side door (at last!). Properly spaced wheels made the revamped Isetta 600 look enough like a conventional car to sell 35,000 more units before giving way to its successor.

We might chuckle, but the little bubble has just about as many roundels on it as its bigger brethren, and it deserves recognition for providing the production volume Munich desperately needed to build the 700-Series cars which would relaunch the company into successful sports car sales once again.

If you want an Isetta, *really* want one, parts are available (see appendix) and cars can be found. Rust is the principal enemy and the later 600's are the most tractable. Still, if you've a sense of humor about the matter, you'll want the incredible egg—no substitute!

Perky, petite and peculiar, the Isetta's staggered rear wheels gave it a three-legged-stool posture. From the side, it's not difficult to realize how the Isetta's "egg" epithet came into play. Interestingly, BMW roundel badges abounded. (David Gooley photo courtesy *Special-Interest Autos*)

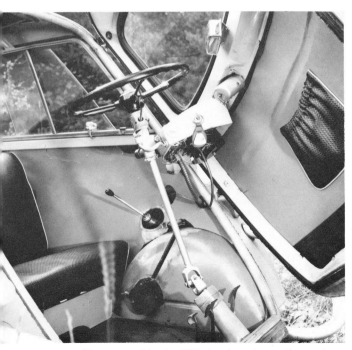

Close-up of Isetta 300 steering shows the motor-cycle shift lever on the left, universal-jointed column and handy, front-door pocket. (Courtesy Michel Potheau and BMWCCA *Roundel*)

A few of the export-model Isettas had single rear wheels and pronounced front nerf bars. (BMW Werkfoto courtesy Halwart Schrader)

Isetta 250/Isetta 300

Engine
Type:................... air-cooled, single cylinder
Bore x Stroke (mm):.............. 68x68 (250), 72x73 (300)
Displacement (cc):..................... 247 (250), 297 (300)
Valve Operation:............................. ohv
Compression Ratio:................. 6.8:1 (250), 7.0:1 (300)
Carburetion:........ one Bing 1/24, one Bing 1/22 (1957-62)
BHP (mfr DIN):............. 12@5800 (250), 13@5200 (300)
Chassis and Drivetrain
Transmission:.......................... 4-speed manual
Steering:............................. worm & nut
Front Suspension:........ leading swing arms, coil springs
Rear Suspension:..... solid axle, quarter-elliptic leaf springs
Axle Ratio:............................. 2.31
General
Wheelbase (mm/in):..................... 1500/59.1
Track front/rear (mm/in):............. 1200/520-47.2/20.5
Brakes:............................. drum/drum
Wheels/Tires:..................... 10x3/4.80-10
Units Produced:.......... 74,312 (1955-62), 84,416 (1956-62)
Maximum speed (kph/mph):................. 85/53
Notes: This 795-lb minicar had two body types in its seven-
year span. Some export versions had a single rear
wheel and raised, high-impact front bumpers.

600

Engine
Type:............... air-cooled, horizontally-opposed twin
Bore x Stroke (mm):............................. 74x68
Displacement (cc):............................. 582
Valve Operation:............................. ohv
Compression Ratio:............................. 6.8:1
Carburetion:..................... one Zenith 28 KLP 1
BHP (mfr DIN):............................. 19.5@4500
Chassis and Drivetrain
Transmission:.......................... 4-speed manual
Steering:............................. worm & nut
Front Suspension:........ leading swing arms, coil springs
Rear Suspension:.......... semitrailing arms, coil springs
Axle Ratio (s):............................. 5.43
General
Wheelbase (mm/in):..................... 1700/66.9
Track front/rear (mm/in):............. 1220/1160-48.0/45.7
Brakes:............................. drum/drum
Wheels/Tires:..................... 10x3½/5.20-10
Units Produced:..................... 34,813 (1957-59)
Maximum Speed (kph/mph):................. 100/62
Notes: The 600 was launched as a 4-passenger variation on
the Isetta. The 600's semitrailing arm rear suspension
became a model for all future BMW's. Very few 600's
were sold in the U.S., still fewer remain.

Steering wheel tilted forward to allow "easy" access. Front bumper guards were standard on export models. Plaid upholstery was yet another cute touch. (David Gooley photo courtesy *Special-Interest Autos*)

Here's the 600's tilt wheel in action. Central shift differentiated this model from bubble predecessors as the 600 was becoming more like a car, less like a motorcycle. (Courtesy Michel Potheau and BMWCCA *Roundel*)

Stylized air intake on 600 was one of numerous tasteful details. Again, BMW badges were proudly displayed. (Courtesy Michel Potheau and BMWCCA *Roundel*)

Purposeful, if a bit small, the 600 brought BMW closer to serious, small-car production. The "limo's" rear seat allowed for additional passengers. (Courtesy Michel Potheau and BMWCCA *Roundel*)

Rear air intake and 600 identifying badge. (Courtesy Michel Potheau and BMWCCA *Roundel*)

Rear passengers entered the 600 via right-hand door. There was adequate space in the rear. (Courtesy Michel Potheau and BMWCCA *Roundel*)

In June 1959, the new 700 (a serious, small car, for a change) began to help BMW recognize a tangible market niche that had been staring at the company all along. The first 700 was an attractive 2+2 coupe, and it was soon joined by a nicely proportioned two-door sedan which afforded a bit more space and style. The 700 still wasn't much larger than the preceding 600, and it used a rear-mounted pancake motorcycle twin, but (and very importantly) it *looked* like a real car. Italian designer Giovanni Michelotti had done his best on this diminutive package. The unit body had adequate space for four passengers, with a reasonably large trunk in front.

The 700's creators smartly considered their new car's powerplant and initially gave the 697 cc air-cooled twin a 30 bhp rating. Sport versions of the coupe and an attractive cabriolet had their compression ratios raised from 7.5 to 9.0:1 and, with twin carburetors, power jumped to 40 bhp.

Sales were encouraging, and in 1961 a longer-wheelbase luxus variant appeared. The following year, recognizing that they had reason to be proud of these little cars, the Müncheners changed the name to BMW LS. In 1963-64 the name was changed to 700CS. Amazingly, 181,121 700's in various guises (including a few tubular-framed mid-engined competition roadsters) were produced before the series ended in 1965.

Sadly, in the 5,000DM range, with bodies built by an outside supplier (Baur of Stuttgart) the cars weren't very profitable. Still they paid their own way and increased market penetration for BMW during an important time period.

It became increasingly evident, confirmed by BMW's market research efforts, that a tempting gap lay between these little cars and the big BMW luxury tourers. But, typical for those days, BMW's planners couldn't agree on the exact product to meet the demand. While they debated, the factory came perilously close to closing, and would have closed had it not been for the 700.

Just as the 700 bowed, stockholders were pressuring the company to sell out to one of the many interested firms. One of these suitors was Daimler-Benz. Being swallowed by the Prussian giant was unthinkable to BMW management, of course.

Financier Harald Quandt, who dabbled in a few automotive risks (the curious Amphicar was one of his unsuccessful flings), bought a great block of BMW stock. His prestigious backing appeased the threats from bankers, creditors and Stuttgarters.

The 700 provided BMW a temporary means to afford tooling for the 1500—generally acknowledged as the car that saved the company. All the credit goes to the 1500, but if it hadn't been for the 700 buying time. . . .

The 700 was an unusual car. It was better to drive than an Isetta or 600 by a long shot. With 40/60 weight distribution, you had to expect some oversteer. Leading links up front and trailing links in back, with coils all around, and a rear roll bar on the sport CS, provided a fairly sophisticated suspension system for the time—and the price class. The 700's rack-and-pinion steering was sure and steady. The gearbox, a four-speed, suffered throughout the model run from balky and imprecise shifting.

The factory raced a series of nineteen lightweight RS model 700's with supertuned, 73 bhp engines. Although their specialty was sprints and hillclimbs, some of the racing 700's were track cars, and they acquitted themselves well. BMW motorcycle tuning was a well-

Moving toward being a full-sized car, the BMW 700 had a more acceptable automotive "look" than the Isetta, although the engine in the 700 was largely adapted from the 600. The Michelotti-designed coupe was attractive and represented good value. This 700 coupe, although a bit tired, attracted a lot of attention at a BMW Oktoberfest. Mirror is a later, nonoriginal addition. (Author photo)

The 700 shared front and rear suspension concept with the 600 but the steel unit-body was all new. (Author photo)

developed art in Germany so many companies offered speed equipment for these little cars. Enthusiasts, on their own, transformed many 700's into fire breathers.

If you're a motorcyclist *and* a Bimmerphile, you'll probably love this little car. While body parts are long gone, engine and gearbox spares are readily available. It's easy to graft on bigger barrels and carburetors to reliably increase power.

All 700's suffer from rust. Fender arches, front panels and taillight housings are the common spots. Still, a well-tuned 700CS sport cabriolet (if you can find one) is a fun car. Driving it in spirited fashion lets you understand just how close BMW was to finding the right combination.

---

700 Coupe and Sedan

Engine
Type:................air-cooled. horizontally-opposed twin
Bore x Stroke (mm): 78x73
Displacement (cc): 697
Valve Operation:................................... ohv
Compression Ratio: 7.5:1
Carburetion: .... one Solex 34 PCI
BHP (mfr DIN): ....30@5000. 32@5000 (1963-64)
Chassis and Drivetrain
Transmission:........................... 4-speed manual
Steering: .... rack & pinion
Front Suspension: .... leading A-arms. coil springs
Rear Suspension:.......... semitrailing arms. coil springs
Axle Ratio:....................................... 5.43
General
Wheelbase (mm/in): 2120/83.5
Track front/rear (mm/in): 1270/1200-50.0/47.2
Brakes:................................... drum/drum
Wheels/Tires:........................12x13½/5.20-12
Units Produced: 23.892 (1959-64), 55.707 (1959-62)
Maximum speed (kph/mph): ...... 125/78 (sedan top speed was 75)
Notes: First BMW with a steel unit-body chassis. The 700 was designed by Giovanni Michelotti.

---

700 Sport/CS Coupe and Convertible

Engine
Type:................air-cooled. horizontally-opposed twin
Bore x Stroke (mm): 78x73
Displacement (cc): 697
Valve Operation:................................... ohv
Compression Ratio: 9.0:1
Carburetion: ....twin Solex 34 PCI
BHP (mfr DIN): ....40@5700
Chassis and Drivetrain
Transmission:........................... 4-speed manual
Steering: .... rack & pinion
Front Suspension: .... leading arms. coil springs
Rear Suspension:... semitrailing arms. coil springs (antiroll bar on sport coupe only)
Axle Ratio:....................................... 5.43
General
Wheelbase (mm/in): 2120/83.5
Track front/rear (mm/in): 1270/1200-50.0/47.2
Brakes:................................... drum/drum
Wheels/Tires: 12x3½/5.20-12. (1963-64) 6.50-12
Units Produced: ... coupe 11.139. convertible 2.592 (1963-64)
Maximum speed (kph/mph): 135/84
Notes: Name was changed in 1964 from 700 Sport to 700CS. These cars were equipped with a rear sway bar and were popular production racers and hillclimbers in Europe. Coupe script on rear fenders identifies sport versions from standard 700's.

The 700 had a very plain dash. (BMW Werkfoto)

700 LS coupe benefited from wheelbase stretch of 6.3 inches. Twin-carburetor, 40 bhp engine aided performance. Stubby look was gone. (BMW Werkfoto)

The 700 coupe had thin front seats for easy rear access. Big taillights were very visible. Thin bumper afforded only scant protection. Exhaust system shown here is not original. (Author photo)

700LS Luxus Sedan and Coupe

Engine
Type: . . . . air-cooled, horizontally-opposed twin
Bore x Stroke (mm): 78x73
Displacement (cc): 697
Valve Operation: . . . . ohv
Compression Ratio: . . . . 7.5:1 (sedan), 9:1 (coupe)
Carburetion: . . one Solex 34 PCI (sedan), twin Solex (coupe)
BHP (mfr DIN): . . . . . . 30@5000 (sedan), after 2/63 32@5000 (sedan), 40@5700 (coupe)

Chassis and Drivetrain
Transmission: . . . . 4-speed manual
Steering: . . . . rack & pinion
Front Suspension: . . . . leading arms, coil springs
Rear Suspension: . . . . semitrailing arms, coil springs
Axle Ratio: 5.43

General
Wheelbase (mm/in): 2280/89.8
Track front/rear (mm/in): 1270/1200-50.0/47.2
Brakes: . . . . drum/drum
Wheels/Tires: 12x3½/5.50-12
Units Produced: 93,061 (1962-65), 1,730 (1964-65)
Maximum speed (kph/mph): 120/75, 135/84
Notes: The 700LS wheelbase was 6.3 inches longer than the 700. The LS coupe was powered by two Solex carburetors. Few were built, as the 700 sport/CS was a better-appointed alternative.

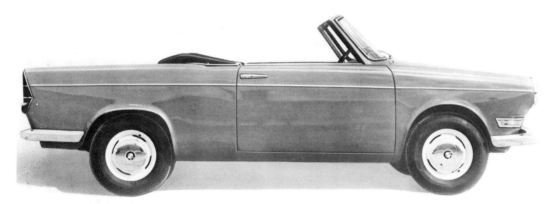

Baur-built 700 sport cabriolet had narrow-bench rear seat, smart lines, very sporty mien. Convertible displayed clean sculpting and low, folding top. It nudged 85 mph. (BMW Werkfoto)

Perky BMW sport 700 looked eager to spring— big headlamps made the front appear almost bug-eyed. (BMW Werkfoto)

Thanks to the wheelbase increase, LX luxus sedan had more room for rear passengers. Luggage space remained the same. (BMW Werkfoto)

BMW sport CS had identifying script on rear fender. The 40 bhp engine and rear antiroll bar helped performance. (BMW Werkfoto)

1500 1962-64 ★★
1600 1964-66 ★★
1800 1963-68 ★★
1800TI 1964-66 ★★
1800TI/SA 1964-65 ★★★✦
1800 1968-72 ★★
2000TI 1966-68 ★★
2000 Tilux 1966-70 ★★
2000tii 1969-72 ★★★

While not yet the answer, the 700 provided sufficient profits for an important range of BMW cars, the 1500 Series. A prototype 1500 aroused favorable comments at the September 1961 Frankfurt show, and the first copies were sold eleven months later. Popularly known at BMW as the New Series, or New Range, the 1500 was truly the car that would save the company.

At last the equation was correct: a medium-sized four-door, five-passenger sedan with an sohc alloy head, high-compression engine. Very acceptable handling, tasteful if not exciting styling and 100 mph autobahn capability (at half the cost of the old 502 V-8) ensured the target market had been squarely hit.

The new 1500 used a BMW body design, although Michelotti had done some helpful consulting. The contemporary, roomy unit body was unmistakably BMW from its slanted twin kidney grilles to its squared-off trunk. Like many good designs, it looked right from the beginning.

Mechanically, the car *glowed*, and set the pattern and pace for today's BMW engineering and design philosophy. From twin front discs to independent suspension, front and rear, this was clearly a driver's car. In fact, the semitrailing, wishbone independent rear suspension was a terrific bonus considering the price range.

Under the hood, another pattern was forming. A willing, oversquare four-cylinder engine, offset thirty degrees, was designed to develop a great percentage of its power for hours of autobahn cruising. An aluminum head, with straight-through porting, five sturdy main bearings and low inertia valve gear held the promise of easy future horsepower and higher revs as the engine was developed.

For a company that had a long trail of marketing mistakes, BMW was beginning to think smartly. For one thing, at least temporarily, the head-to-head competition with Mercedes-Benz was over. The 1500 was all by itself in the German market, and, for that matter, the world. Not surprisingly, export sales began to pick up. In the US, Max Hoffman finally had a car he could really get behind.

The interior, while simple, was tastefully done. The package had plenty of space for people and luggage. It represented wonderful value in the now-recovered German economy.

In just two and one-half years, BMW built 23,807 1500's. The car's success encouraged the Müncheners to think even bigger. In the fall of 1963, the 1800 appeared, closely followed in the spring by the 1600. Building the 1800 involved increasing the bore and stroke (to 84 x 80 mm) in the very versatile new motor. Even with one Solex, power was up to 90 bhp.

The 1600 was a variation that kept the 1500's stroke and added the 1800's bigger pistons for an 84x71 mm combination, with only seven fewer horsepower. Another permutation, the 2000, bowed in 1966—with an 89x80 mm bore and stroke, 1990 cc and a full 100 bhp. Exteriors, except for minor trim and identification details, were substantially the same, although slight facelifting took place each year.

The 1500 introduction ushered in a new era of prosperity for BMW. The new car's clean lines, fresh engineering and spritely sohc four laid down the pattern of BMW's to come for many years. (BMW Werkfoto courtesy Halwart Schrader)

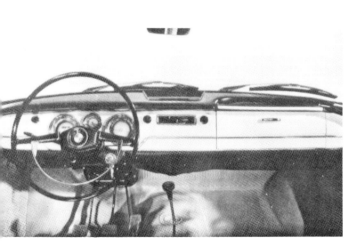

The 1500's dash was plain but functional. To install a radio, it was necessary to cut into the panel or, more easily, install the unit below the dash. (BMW Werkfoto courtesy Halwart Schrader)

Clean front appearance was yet another 1500 plus. The twin kidney grilles were back to stay on BMW passenger cars. (BMW Werkfoto courtesy Halwart Schrader)

It wasn't long before BMW's sport-minded engineers began to add carburetion to their very willing new engine. Simultaneous with the 1800's introduction in 1963, a sports version, the 1800 TI (Touring International), began to excite enthusiasts. Twin Solexes and a bump in compression yielded 110 bhp. A year and a half later, in January 1965, the 1800 TI/SA proved BMW's engineers really meant business.

The TI/SA (you could pick one of three meanings: Sonderaustatung, Special Equipment; Sportausfuhring, Sports Version; or Speciale Analage, Touring International) was a thinly disguised competition wolf in street sheep's clothing. The TI/SA was originally available only for competition license holders. Interestingly, Michel Potheau notes that Max Hoffman, despite his dislike of motorsports, produced a mailing on the car to all Sports Car Club of America (SCCA) license holders in the US.

Under the hood, this Munich menace sported big 45DCOE Webers, 10.5:1 compression and a 130 bhp rating. The sedan's performance was remarkable for the era: 0-60 in nine seconds and a top end of over 120 mph.

The TI configuration, with appropriate trunk script, was available in 1600 and 2000 versions with 105 and 120 bhp, respectively. And, the 1600 TI came in a two-door version which inspired later generations of BMW supercoupes.

No other TI/SA variants were forthcoming. The 1600 engine was beginning to reach the limit of its development and the factory had interesting plans for the 2000, as we shall see.

As sales continued to increase in 1966, the 2000 TI Lux, more popularly known as the Tilux, made its appearance. The Tilux's leather interior, walnut dash and upmarket trim provided all the comfort befitting a top-of-the-line entry. *Autoweek*'s John L. Matras, in a retrospective piece, called it, "a sports car for someone with friends." Matras found the Tilux to be more than a pleasant memory: "Find the roughest road you know: Forty year old concrete, cracked broken and rudely patched. Knife-edged ridges and holes. A road that rattles and shakes the torque out of every nut and bolt of a normal car, Locktite and all.

"Drive the BMW 2000 Tilux there first. The ride will astound you, supple and smooth, and you will drive down that road faster than you ever have before. The BMW soaks it all up and asks for more. You might be tempted to believe that it's all cushy shocks and springs, but there's more.

"Change the venue. A winding road, bituminous velvet unrolling like a memory over and around rounded hills and farms with white painted fences, thoroughbreds and horses to be rode [sic] to the hounds. Work the Bimmer through the gears, twisting it to redline, letting it whine like a lathe spinning out horsepower turned from the solid billet. Brake for a corner and discover that you've been traveling at almost double the posted limit. In complete safety."

The final stroke in this rapid sedan series was the 2000tii in 1969. This road rocket with a 130 bhp Kugelfischer injected four packed an optional five-speed and would menace the autobahn at speeds topping 115. The tii was BMW's first production use of fuel injection—it would not be the last.

Picking a car from this series, if you can find one in good condition, is an easy choice for an enthusiast; the TI/SA, Tilux and tii are the ones to covet. Still, the "cooking" sedans, from a historical standpoint, are also interesting. Weak spots are the gearbox and a lack of spare sheet metal. Strong points are the eager engine, the brakes (the second-series 1968 1800's received a split braking system with four-piston front calipers) and handling well above par for period four-door sedans. The people in Stuttgart were beginning to take notice.

```
                        1500
Engine
Type:......................... in-line, water-cooled 4
Bore x Stroke (mm):........................ 82x71
Displacement (cc):............................ 1499
Valve Operation:.............................. sohc
Compression Ratio:........................... 8.8:1
Carburetion: .... one Solex 34 PCIB. Solex 36-40 PDSI (1964)
BHP (mfr DIN):.......................... 80@5700
Chassis and Drivetrain
Transmission:...................... 4-speed manual
Steering: ........................... worm & roller
Front Suspension: ........ MacPherson struts. coil springs
Rear Suspension:.......... semitrailing arms. coil springs
Axle Ratio:................................... 4.375
General
Wheelbase (mm/in):................... 2550/100.4
Track front/rear (mm/in):......... 1320/1366-52.0/53.8
Brakes:.................................. disc/drum
Wheels/Tires:........ 14x4½J/6.00-14 (165SR-14 optional)
Units Produced:.................... 23.807 (1962-64)
Maximum speed (kph/mph):................ 148/92
Notes: New with the 1500. the MacPherson strut front sus-
       pension would continue indefinitely. An all-new sohc 4
       design laid a pattern for all BMW engines to follow.
```

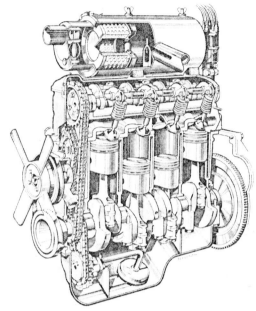

All-new with the 1500 was a 1499 cc chain-driven sohc engine. Its 80 bhp was increased with changes in cylinder size, compression ratios, carburetors and camshafts as the years passed. (BMW drawing)

The 1600 represented a lot of improvements over the 1500. Besides the 2 mm bore increase and 3 bhp additions, considerable attention to engineering details was evident upon close examination. (BMW Werkfoto)

Rear view of the 1600 duplicated the 1500, save for the new badge. Practical bumper guards were cleanly integrated. (BMW Werkfoto courtesy Halwart Schrader)

1600	
Engine	
Type:.....................	in-line water-cooled 4
Bore x Stroke (mm):...........................	84x71
Displacement (cc):...........................	1573
Valve Operation:...........................	sohc
Compression Ratio:...........................	8.6:1
Carburetion:.....................	one Solex 36-40 PDSI
BHP (mfr DIN):...........................	83@5500
Chassis and Drivetrain	
Transmission:...........................	4-speed manual
Steering:...........................	worm & roller
Front Suspension:.........	MacPherson struts. coil springs
Rear Suspension:.........	semitrailing arms. coil springs
Axle Ratio:...........................	4.275
General	
Wheelbase (mm/in):...........................	2550/100.4
Track front/rear (mm/in):...........	1320/1366-52.0/53.8
Brakes:...........................	disc/drum
Wheels/Tires:....... 14x4½J/6.00S-14 (165SR-14 optional)	
Units Produced: ...9.728 (1964-66). some sources say 10.278	
Maximum speed (kph/mph):...........................	155/96
Notes: The 1600 succeeded the 1500: 2 mm bore increase added 3 hp. No external differences. save badges. marked the model transition.	

First-series 1800's (1963-68) quickly eclipsed the 1500 and 1600 models in sales. The TI designation indicated a 20 bhp increase over the standard 1800 due to twin Solexes. Gearboxes on these cars were problematical. (BMW Werkfoto courtesy Halwart Schrader)

1800	
Engine	
Type:...........................	in-line. water-cooled 4
Bore x Stroke (mm):...........................	89x71
Displacement (cc):...........................	1766
Valve Operation:...........................	sohc
Compression Ratio:...........................	8.6:1
Carburetion:.....................	one Solex 36-40 PDSI
BHP (mfr DIN):...........................	90@5250
Chassis and Drivetrain	
Transmission:..4-speed manual or (1966) 3-speed automatic	
Steering:...........................	worm & roller
Front Suspension:.........	MacPherson struts. coil springs
Rear Suspension:.........	semitrailing arms. coil springs
Axle Ratio:...........................	4.11 (4.22 automatic)
General	
Wheelbase (mm/in):...........................	2550/100.4
Track front/rear (mm/in):...........	1330/1376-52.4/54.2
Brakes:...........................	disc/drum
Wheels/Tires:...........	14x5J. 6.45/1655-14
Units Produced:...........................	39.020 (1968-72)
Maximum speed (kph/mph):...........................	166/103
Notes: In April 1971. a second-series 1800 incorporated blacked-out grilles. improved dual-circuit brakes. rectangular headlights and a revised instrument panel.	

This simple side elevation of the 1800 shows the main difference marking this car from its New Series predecessors: a chrome strip along the rocker panel. (BMW Werkfoto)

The 1800's newly restyled dash had a raised center section, hooded instrument grouping, central heating and ventilation controls, and a dished steering wheel. (BMW Werkfoto courtesy Halwart Schrader)

1800 identification badge on the new second-series 1800 moved to the right side above the taillights. Wider, horizontal lights were a change from the earlier car's vertical units. (BMW Werk-foto)

The second-series 1800 (1968-72) was distinguished from the earlier 1800 by a partially blacked-out grille along with satin finish (versus brightly chromed) hubcaps. Its 90 bhp output pushed the sedan to just over the 100 mph mark—and the car would run for hours at high speeds. (BMW Werkfoto)

1800/1800TI

Engine

Type:................................ in-line water-cooled 4
Bore x Stroke (mm):............................ 84x80
Displacement (cc):................................1773
Valve Operation:................................... sohc
Compression Ratio:........................ 8.6:1. 9.5:1 (TI)
Carburetion: ...one Solex 36-40 PDSI. two Solex 40 PHH (TI)
BHP (mfr DIN):................. 90@5250. 110@5800 (TI)

Chassis and Drivetrain

Transmission:........4-speed manual or 3-speed automatic
Steering: .... worm & roller
Front Suspension: MacPherson struts. coil springs. optional antiroll bar
Rear Suspension:..semi-trailing arms. coil springs. optional antiroll bar
Axle Ratio:............... 4.22 (auto 4.11) 4.11 or 3.89 (TI)

General

Wheelbase (mm/in): 2550/100.4
Track front/rear (mm/in): .. 1320/1366-52.0/53.8. 1330/1376-52.0/54.2 (TI)
Brakes:................................. disc/drum
Wheels/Tires: ...... 14x4½J/6.00S-14. 14x5JK/6.00S-14 (TI)
Units Produced: ..... 102.090 (1963-68). 19.663 (TI. 1964-66)
Maximum speed (kph/mph): .... 162/100. 175/109 (TI)
Notes: An additional model. the 1800TI/SA. was available from 1964-66 in a series of 200 cars sold only to licensed racers. These special versions had 10.5:1 compression. twin Weber carburetors. 130 bhp. sway bars front and rear and an optional limited slip differential. Rear end ratio choices were: 4.11. 4.22. 4.75 or 5.86. Top speed was 116 mph.

Horizontal headlamps and a chromed grille surround highlighted the 2000 in February 1966. The single-carburetor 2000 had an optional ZF three-speed automatic.(BMW Werkfoto)

Automatic-equipped 2000's were distinguished from the rear with a special script. This rare example appeared at a recent BMW Oktoberfest gathering. (Author photo)

The 2000 TI could be driven aggressively, as this example in the US is demonstrating. The TI/Tilux had twin carburetors for a 120 bhp output and a 111 mph top speed (wheels are not original on this car). (Yale Rachlin photo)

In Germany, TI's had horizontal headlights (illegal in the US) but most other details remained the same. (BMW Werkfoto courtesy Richard O. Neville)

Seen from the rear, "cooking" 2000's shape is pleasing. (BMW Werkfoto courtesy Halwart Schrader)

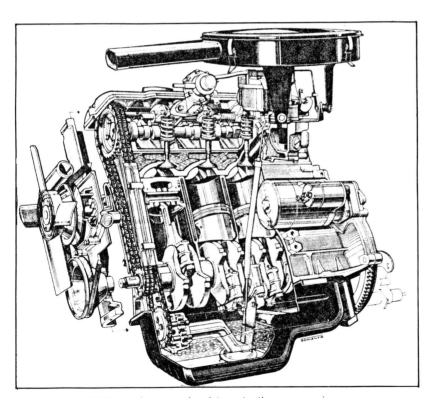

The 100-bhp 2000 engine remained true to the new series concept. Its big-bore/short stroke relationship facilitated high-speed cruising. (BMW drawing)

The 2000tii had Kugelfischer mechanical fuel injection replacing twin Solexes. Other details to note were slotted wheels, HR-rated tires. The tii, with 130 bhp, would top 115. It was the first production BMW with fuel injection. (BMW Werkfoto)

2000

Engine
Type:. . . . . in-line. water-cooled 4
Bore x Stroke (mm): 89x80
Displacement (cc): 1990
Valve Operation:. . . . . sohc
Compression Ratio: 8.5:1
Carburetion: . . . . one Solex 40 PDSI
BHP (mfr DIN): . . . . 100@5500

Chassis and Drivetrain
Transmission:. . . . . . . .4-speed manual or 3-speed automatic
Steering: . . . . worm & roller
Front Suspension: . . . . MacPherson struts. coil springs
(optional antiroll bar)
Rear Suspension:. . . . . semitrailing arms. coil springs
(optional antiroll bar)
Axle Ratio:. 4.11

General
Wheelbase (mm/in): 2550/100.4
Track front/rear (mm/in): 1330/1376-52.4/54.2
Brakes:. . . . . disc/drum
Wheels/Tires: . . . . 14x5J/6.45/1655-14 or 165SR-14
Units Produced: 120.495 (1966-72)
Maximum speed (kph/mph): 168/104
Notes: This model is recognizable by its wide-band headlights
and horizontal taillights. A twin-carburetor TI version
was available. The three-speed automatic was only
available with the single carburetor engine.

2000TI/tilux. 2000tii

Engine
Type:. . . . . in-line. water-cooled 4
Bore x Stroke (mm): 89x80
Displacement (cc): 1990
Valve Operation:. . . . . sohc
Compression Ratio: . . . . 9.3:1. 9.5:1 (tii)
Carburetion: . . . two Solex 40 PHH. Kugelfischer mechanical
fuel injection (tii)
BHP (mfr DIN): . . . . 120@5500. 130@5800 (tii)

Chassis and Drivetrain
Transmission:. . . . . 4-speed manual
Steering: . . . . worm & roller
Front Suspension: . . . . MacPherson struts. coil springs.
antiroll bar
Rear Suspension:. . . . . semitrailing arms. coil springs.
antiroll bar
Axle Ratio:. 3.90

General
Wheelbase (mm/in): 2550/100.4
Track front/rear (mm/in): 1330/1376-52.4/54.2
Brakes:. . . . . disc/drum
Wheels/Tires: . . . . 14x5½J/6.95/75H-14. 175HR-14. 1755SR or
HR-14 (tii)
Units Produced: . . . . . . 17.440 (TI 1966-70). 1.922 (tii 1969-72)
Maximum speed (kph/mph): . . . . 180/111. 185/115 (tii)
Notes: In 1968. the TI-lux designation became tilux. The 2000tii.
BMW's first fuel-injected production model. appeared
in late 1969.

<table>
<tr><td>1502 1975-77</td><td>★★</td></tr>
<tr><td>1600-2/1602 1966-75</td><td>★★★</td></tr>
<tr><td>1600 Cabriolet 1967-71</td><td>★★★★</td></tr>
<tr><td>1600 Touring 1971-72</td><td>★★★</td></tr>
<tr><td>1600 Ti 1967-68</td><td>★★★</td></tr>
<tr><td>1802 1971-75</td><td>★★★</td></tr>
<tr><td>1800 Touring 1971-74</td><td>★★★</td></tr>
<tr><td>2002 1968-75</td><td>★★★</td></tr>
<tr><td>2002 Cabriolet 1971-75</td><td>★★★★</td></tr>
<tr><td>2000 Touring 1971-74</td><td>★★★</td></tr>
<tr><td>2002ti 1968-71</td><td>★★★★</td></tr>
<tr><td>2002ti 1971-75</td><td>★★★★</td></tr>
<tr><td>2002tii 1971-75</td><td>★★★★</td></tr>
<tr><td>2002tii Touring 1971-74</td><td>★★★★</td></tr>
</table>

CHAPTER 8
1600-2/2002,
2002ti, 2002tii

In March 1966, BMW introduced a car that would dramatically affect its fortunes. Fast on the heels of the six-cylinder 2500 Series would come a second success in the form of an innocent-appearing 85 bhp two-door sedan called, in Germany, the 1600-2.

While BMW family resemblance was both marked and intentional, the little two-door was smaller in all dimensions than its 1600 four-door predecessor, and 500 pounds lighter. As a result, performance was up and the added sales reflected the public's quick response to this nifty little rejuggling of basic BMW components in a new package.

At the Frankfurt show in September of the following year, a 105 bhp twin-carb version, the TI, was offered. The reaction, while predictable, was unprecedented. In the US, up until this time, BMW had received rather indifferent acceptance despite the best efforts of importer Max Hoffman. Hoffman, who at various times had been responsible for an extraordinary parade of foreign makes, had a special fondness and persistence for BMW—and this little 1600-2 would see his persistence pay off.

Road & Track testers quickly caught on: "It winds smoothly right through the rev range and is still pulling eagerly at the 6000 rpm redline. In fact, it wanted to go to 6500, but we decided to respect the book for our tests . . . we were frankly surprised at the high level of performance we discovered . . . The suspension is no less than excellent . . . at the same time, the car's excellent handling and stability aren't achieved at the expense of a comfortable ride . . . Detroit simply isn't in the same league . . . At the risk of becoming tiresome, let us say just once more that the BMW 1600 is a great automobile at the price."

Calling the 1600 "The best small sedan we ever drove," *Car and Driver* editors, never at a loss for words when praises (or curses) were deserved, said the 1600 ". . . was like driving a 1300cc Alfa Veloce built by Germans." All over the car, they found things to like: "The bright metal is tastefully laid on and it looks like it'll last. Every piece is straight, every piece fits, and the quality of finish is universally excellent.

"Doors, hood and trunk-lid all convey a substantial Mercedes-ish feeling of heft, durability and perfect fit. It's a definite tactile pleasure to open and close anything from a door to an ashtray. They all click, snap, thump, latch and lock with the same reassuring mechanical precision that one gets from a Leica. . . ."

The test is vintage *Car and Driver*: "Floor the throttle and it takes off like a scalded dog. Point it into a corner, any corner, and unless you've simply lost your mind, it'll track

Here's how the thrills began: The 1600 two-door had all the punch of the New Range sedans in a lightweight, great-handling little coupe. The term sports car was about to be redefined. Note the clean dash and purposeful front end. (BMW Werkfoto)

around like it was locked into a slot." The cover summed it all up in big letters: "The world's best $2500 automobile."

The normally staid British roadtesters had their chance earlier. O.G.W. Fersen of *Autocar* said: "Roadholding may be termed exceptional and repeatedly the car went through tight bends on a winding tarmac road in perfectly controllable four-wheel drifts . . . the new 1600 looks in no way a cheap version of the four-door saloon . . . it is a well-built car . . . offering an exhilarating performance at what promises to be a reasonable price!"

The reasons for the 1600's success were simple: It was a light, quick, well-made car. It outclassed everything in its price range on the road and took advantage of a then very favorable Deutschmark-to-dollar ratio.

But Hoffman had still another ace up his sleeve. To counter the US emissions regulations, and to increase his already hot little two-door's performance, he asked Munich to install its single-carburetor two-liter four in the 1600, and the 2002 was born. BMW sales edged ahead even further.

The new 1600 and 2002 redefined the term "practical sports cars" for many buyers. You simply didn't need a topless two-seater anymore. The 2002 would run rings around M.G.'s, Datsuns and the like—with four occupants seated quite comfortably. Almost overnight, roadtest raves turned the 2002 into a cult car. Although imitators began their efforts, BMW had a terrific head start.

For the family who wanted a sporty car, the 2002 neatly struck a compromise. You could run it all day at top speed, flogging its slick gearbox; or run it sedately to a formal affair, lugging in traffic all day if need be, without the temperature gauge protesting.

Typically for BMW, it only took ten months for the company to market the first hot-rod version, the 2002TI. Packing 120 bhp, the TI and its hotter injected successor, the tii (introduced in April 1971), were the cars enthusiasts then, and collectors now, all agree upon.

When the 2002 first appeared, roadtesters, who had driven European versions at first, were excited about what over twenty-seven percent more torque could do for the 1600 in a car weighing only eight percent (160 pounds) more. Sadly, as *Road & Track* discovered when it finally tested the Americanized versions, something had been lost. "But apparently the emission control system—air injection with the usual carbureton-distributor changes—has taken its toll and the 2002 just barely tops the acceleration figures of the 1600 we tested last year." The writers went on to point out that 1968 1600's, *with* emission controls, were probably slower than the previous year's cars, too.

Road & Track felt the 2002 ". . . is also noisier than the 1600 and feels somewhat under-geared at high cruising speeds." On the plus side, "The noises, from the enthusiast's viewpoint, are all pleasant ones—from the characteristic BMW camdrive whine heard at low speeds to the sound of a healthy engine sailing right past its redline without a clatter."

Interestingly, the editors liked the 1600 as "the best value in the BMW line."

Overseas, with unfettered engines, *Motor* editors were more enthusiastic. "So now BMW have joined the shoehorn bandwagon, the fashionable habit of putting your larger engine into a smaller chassis; and what admirable transport this makes the 2002." Commenting on the higher final-drive ratio fitted to the 2002 (in Europe and overseas), the writers felt this gave ". . . pleasantly long-legged touring and really useful maxima in the gears." *Motor*'s summation: "Few cars manage to have such a character variation but play each part so well; we thought it an outstanding car."

In late 1969, the 2002 was fitted with an automatic. Enthusiasts cringed, but they needn't have worried. BMW's addition of the three-speed ZF automatic (already available in the 2000-Series sedans) was far from a retrograde step. Testers found very little was lost: The 0.3-second difference in quarter-mile times was minor compared to the automatic's smoothness and tractability.

Road & Track was annoyed at the popular BMW practice of adding on every conceivable extra which, in its opinion, raised the price of the 2002A to an unacceptable(!) $3,679 . . . from

The Touring 1600 offered a practical variation on the two-door's design theme. The hatchback, while useful, never achieved the coupe's sales volume. (BMW Werkfoto)

Clean, crisp, well-defined and agile, the 85 bhp 1600 was a lot of car for the money. (BMW Werkfoto)

a base of $3,340. The add-ons included radial tires ($59), vinyl upholstery ($45), chrome exhaust tip ($2), reclining seats ($48), power brakes ($45), antiroll bars ($20), tachometer ($40) and the ever-present dealer prep ($40).

Autocar's John Bolster called the 2002A an "automatic with a sporting character," and reveled in the car's ability to retain its high-performance nature with the smoothness of automatic shifting.

Although European customers could enjoy the twin-carburetor TI, Americans who wanted more performance had to wait until 1971 for the 2002tii as the powerplant that would meet the ever more stringent US emission regulations. When the 2002tii bowed, BMW discontinued the 1600 and a mild facelift distinguished the two 2002 versions in the US.

The external differences were minor: Wider, rubber-tipped bumpers, a rubber-faced body molding, newly shaped front seats and some instrument panel revisions rounded off the changes. The big news was under the hood where, for about $400 extra, performance buyers found a Kugelfischer mechanical fuel-injection system. This unit provided nearly thirty pounds-feet more torque, peaking between 4000 and 4700 rpm (versus the 2002's torque peak of 3000). The power was there—you just had to rev the very willing engine. From the 2002TI, the tii got 1.4 inches additional track, front and rear, H-rated Michelin XAS's, wider wheels and bigger brakes.

A new four-speed gearbox was standard, and a five-speed option was available (the scarce five-speed is nearly impossible to find today). The tii felt like a 2002 in all aspects below 4000 rpm. After that, look out! The car definitely had the "right stuff" and times in every category were bettered. *Road & Track* comparison tested the tii against the Alfa 1750 Berlina and the Mazda RX-2. The BMW was the clear winner, but it was pointed out that the German car was considerably ($1,400) more expensive. The Japanese cars were beginning to make inroads, and comments on value for money (as BMW's prices increased) were beginning to be heard.

The 2002 received a lower compression ratio (from 8.5 to 8.3:1) in 1972 and a number of other emasculating emissions changes were felt, lowering the car's performance potential. The factory, copying its six-cylinder cars, introduced the trispherical combustion-chamber heads in 1973 and helped restore the lost urge. Lean carburetion surges were gone and the 2002 was back to its old fast tricks.

In Europe, the inevitable 1802 appeared in 1971 and the 1600-2 was called simply 1602. BMW was beginning to feel the pressures of Department of Transportation (DOT) and Environmental Protection Agency (EPA) regulations, so while US 1600/2002 cars could be equipped with optional sunroofs, the convertible cabriolet versions of these cars marketed in Europe made rare appearances on US shores.

Baur Karosserie produced 1,682 cabrios from 1967-71, and these cars command a premium among collectors. The basic mechanical specs are unchanged, but the convertibles are two inches shorter than the coupes. Baur also built a targa version of the 02 Series which incorporated a sunroof and a convertible rear windscreen. This was a not-too-attractive variant that sold in small numbers overseas and is an extremely rare model in the US. As a note for collectors, these drop-top Bimmers are certainly unusual, but they're not worth colossal premiums, so be careful. At a gathering of BMW aficionados, however, you're sure to be a star if you roll up with the top down.

BMW presented another body variation which appeared in January 1971, and sadly heralded one of the company's few marketing errors during this expansion period. The cars, known as Touring hatchbacks, were confusingly called 1600, 1800 and 2000 for a few years —and there was a tii version of the two-liter car. In 1972, the company reverted to the common designations 1602, 1802, 2002 and 2002tii.

Ahead of its time, the curious-looking hatchback never sold well. Its sales volume of 29,230 was less than six percent of the 1600/2002 total of 499,479.

From the rear, the Baur 1600 convertible was equally neat. These cars were only rarely imported into the US; they're of great interest to collectors today. (Author photo)

1502
Engine
Type:................................. in-line. water-cooled 4
Bore x Stroke (mm): 84x71
Displacement (cc): 1573
Valve Operation:................................... sohc
Compression Ratio: 8.0:1
Carburetion: .... one Solex 38 PDSI
BHP (mfr DIN): ....75@5800
Chassis and Drivetrain
Transmission:......................... 4-speed manual
Steering: .... worm & roller
Front Suspension: .... MacPherson struts. coil springs
Rear Suspension:.......... semitrailing arms. coil springs
Axle Ratio:.. 4.11
General
Wheelbase (mm/in): 2500/98.4
Track front/rear (mm/in): 1330/1330-52.4/52.4
Brakes:...................................... disc/drum
Wheels/Tires: 13x4½J/165SR-13
Units Produced: ..72.635 (1975-77). some sources say 71.564
Maximum speed (kph/mph): 157/97
Notes: BMW's oil-crisis fighter. a bare-bones coupe. was not sold in North America. but was popular in Europe. Sales continued even after the new 3-Series was introduced.

1600-2/1602, 1600ti
Engine
Type:................................. in-line. water-cooled 4
Bore x Stroke (mm): 84x71
Displacement (cc): 1573
Valve Operation:................................... sohc
Compression Ratio: .... 8.6:1. 9.5:1 (ti)
Carburetion: ..... one Solex 38 PDSI. twin Solex 40 PHH (ti)
BHP (mfr DIN): .... 85@5700. 105@6000 (ti)
Chassis and Drivetrain
Transmission:.... 4-speed manual. 4- or 5-speed manual (ti)
Steering: .... worm & roller
Front Suspension: .... MacPherson struts. coil springs
Rear Suspension:.......... semitrailing arms. coil springs
Axle Ratio:............................. 4.11. 3.90 (ti)
General
Wheelbase (mm/in): 2500/98.4
Track front/rear (mm/in): 1330/1330-52.4/52.4
Brakes:...................................... disc/drum
Wheels/Tires: .... 13x4½J/165S-13: after August 1970. 165SR-13
Units Produced: 277.320 (1966-72)
Maximum speed (kph/mph): .... 162/100. 175/109 (ti)
Notes: The Baur convertibles were rarely imported into the US. The twin-carburetor ti was introduced in September 1967. Antiroll bars. front and rear. were optional on the ti.

Higher EPA standards saw the US tii gradually lose horsepower. The European car had 150, early US models had 140 but by 1973 horsepower was down to 125. In 1974, with the addition of safety bumpers, the heavier, slower 2002 and 2002tii awaited relief from the new 3-Series.

In Europe, where the OPEC gasoline madness of 1973-74 had a very strong effect, BMW kept producing the 02-Series cars in 1975 alongside the new 3-Series. That meant Continental buyers could have a low-buck, low-compression 1573 cc, 75 bhp 1502 for 2,000DM less than the new 3-Series cars. For two and one-half years, with sales that topped 72,000, the 1502 was available as a bottom-of-the-line bargain carryover . . . presumably until Munich's marketing experts were truly satisfied that their new car had a firm foothold in the marketplace.

From today's perspective, the 1600 and 2002 still represent attractive buys—with some qualifications. Since many die-hard Bimmerphiles still think BMW stopped making good (read affordable) cars when the 02's bowed out, firms such as Automotive Import Recycling, Inc. (AIR), of Belvidere, New Jersey, are doing a thriving business rebuilding 1600's and 2002's. They'll even update the cars with aftermarket suspensions, four-wheel discs, engine modifications, Recaros and so on. AIR currently charges a base of $9,750 to remanufacture a 1972-74 tii and does it at a rate of twenty cars a month.

Before you rush your old 02 to the restoration shop, consider what a like investment will do for you with a used 320. Driving a 2002 today reminds you of just how far BMW has come, particularly in terms of suspension sophistication. The old cars feel rough, Spartan; sporty, it's true, but years of refinement have smoothed everything out on the newer cars. Of course, a well-tuned 2002tii will take the measure of a 320, so with prices climbing, money invested in a solid 02 is probably well spent. The 2002 versus 320 controversy will probably be settled with the 325e rocket variant in 1984—if only it still cost $4,000!

1802/1800 Touring

Engine

Type: . . . . in-line, water-cooled 4
Bore x Stroke (mm): 89x71
Displacement (cc): 1766
Valve Operation: . . . . sohc
Compression Ratio: 8.6:1
Carburetion: . . . . one Solex 38 PDSI
BHP (mfr DIN): . . . . 90@5250

Chassis and Drivetrain

Transmission: . . . . 4-speed manual
Steering: . . . . worm & roller
Front Suspension: . . . . MacPherson struts, coil springs, antiroll bar*
Rear Suspension: . . . . semitrailing arms, coil springs, antiroll bar
Axle Ratio: 4.11

General

Wheelbase (mm/in): 2500/98.4
Track front/rear (mm/in): 1330/1330-52.4/52.4
Brakes: . . . . disc/drum
Wheels/Tires: 13x4½J (1973-75, 13x5J), 165SR-13
Units Produced: . . . 83,351 (1971-75), 3,099 Touring (1971-74)
Maximum speed (kph/mph): . . . . 167/104, 165/102 (Touring)
Notes: These models were not sold in North America.
*Optional on 1802, standard on 1800 Touring.

58

Another ragtop variation (Baur-bodied), the 1602 convertible, was available from 1967-71. Alloy wheels and twin exhaust weren't standard. Side-marker lights indicate this car was prepared for sale in the US. (Author photo)

The 90 bhp 1802 was not available in North America. A 5 mm bore increase upped the displacement. (BMW Werkfoto)

The 2002 was a clever solution to emissions control regulations. Rather than muzzle a twin-carburetor 1600TI, simply drop in a bigger engine. Side lamps mark this car as an export model. (BMW Werkfoto)

2002 Coupe/2002 Cabriolet/2000 Touring

Engine

Type:	in-line, water-cooled 4
Bore x Stroke (mm):	89x80
Displacement (cc):	1990
Valve Operation:	sohc
Compression Ratio:	8.5:1
Carburetion:	one Solex 40PDSI (In 1973, US cars used a Solex 2-bbl carburetor)
BHP (mfr DIN):	100@5500

Chassis and Drivetrain

Transmission:	4-speed manual or 3-speed automatic, later 5-speed manual
Steering:	worm & roller
Front Suspension:	MacPherson struts, coil springs, antiroll bar*
Rear Suspension:	semitrailing arms, coil springs, antiroll bar*
Axle Ratio:	3.64

General

Wheelbase (mm/in):	2500/98.4
Track front/rear (mm/in):	1330/1330-52.4/52.4
Brakes:	disc/drum
Wheels/Tires:	13x4½J/165SR-13
Units Produced:	339,084 coupe (1968-76), 4,199 cabriolet (1971-75), 5,705 Touring (1971-74)
Maximum speed (kph/mph):	173/107

Notes: A 1971 facelift modernized the 2002's appearance: new side trim, redesigned bumpers and trim. The best-selling single BMW in its time. The 2002 firmly established Munich's high-performance reputation. In 1974, US cars received 5 mph bumpers. These added 200 lbs to the car's weight and 9.5 inches to its length. In Europe, the Baur conversion convertible was available, weighing 110 lbs more than the coupe. 2000 Tourings had driving lights as standard equipment.

* Roll bar optional on Cabriolet.

Rear view of the US 2002. Back-up lights were an option, along with sturdy bumper guards. (BMW Werkfoto)

This German 2002's license lighting differs from the export version. Lacking side-marker lights, this car was the second 2002 version built following a 1971 facelift. (BMW Werkfoto)

1974 2002 changes for North America included restyled, slotted five-inch wheels, 5-mph-impact bumpers. Sadly, these changes added 9.5 inches to the car's length and nearly 200 pounds. (BMW Werkfoto)

The Baur 2002 cabriolet introduced in Europe in 1971. Rear portion of top folded down and midsection was removable. The result? Open-air motoring with the safety of a built-in roll bar. The weight penalty was about 110 pounds. (BMW Werkfoto)

2002TI *seetix*

Engine
Type:........................... in-line. water-cooled 4
Bore x Stroke (mm): 89x80
Displacement (cc): 1990
Valve Operation:.................................... sohc
Compression Ratio: 9.3:1
Carburetion: .... twin Solex 40 PHH
BHP (mfr DIN): ....120@5500
Chassis and Drivetrain
Transmission: .... 4- or 5-speed manual
Steering: .... worm & roller
Front Suspension: .... MacPherson struts. coil springs. antiroll bars
Rear Suspension: ......semitrailing arms. coil springs. anti-roll bars
Axle Ratio:................................ 3.64
General
Wheelbase (mm/in): 2500/98.4
Track front/rear (mm/in): 1342/1342-52.8/52.8
Brakes:.................................... disc/drum
Wheels/Tires: 13x5J/165HR-13
Units Produced: 16.448 (1968-71)
Maximum speed (kph/mph): 185/115
Notes: Not exported to North America: front and rear antiroll bars were standard.

View of the late-model Baur 2002 convertible. With the top and midsections removed, there was lots of breeze. Extended bumpers really lengthened the car, as you can see when you compare this photo to the earlier Baur conversions. (BMWCCA photo courtesy Yale Rachlin)

For Europe only, the 2002TI had a twin-Solex-equipped 120 bhp engine. The car was not officially imported into the US. (BMW Werkfoto)

European 2000 Touring was built in this and 2000tii configurations from 1971-72. After 1973, the Touring designations matched the rest of the line with the 1802 and the 2002. The 1.6 liter variant ceased production in 1972. Full hubcaps distinguished the 2000. (BMW Werkfoto)

Two views of a 2002tii Touring. This car had the required US side lights and has been tastefully modified with BBS wheels, front air dam, lowered suspension and a turbocharger. Careful modifications like these will generally not detract from a car's resale value too much, but a 2002 Touring in stock form would be worth more in comparable condition. (Author photos)

2002tii/Touring	
Engine	
Type:	in-line, water-cooled 4
Bore x Stroke (mm):	89x80
Displacement (cc):	1990
Valve Operation:	sohc
Compression Ratio:	9.5:1
Carburetion:	Kugelfischer mechanical fuel injection
BHP (mfr DIN):	130@5800
Chassis and Drivetrain	
Transmission:	4- or 5-speed manual
Steering:	worm & roller
Front Suspension:	MacPherson struts, coil springs, antiroll bar
Rear Suspension:	semi-trailing arms, coil springs, antiroll bar
Axle Ratio:	3.64
General	
Wheelbase (mm/in):	2500/98.4
Track front/rear (mm/in):	1342/1342-52.8/52.8
Brakes:	disc/drum
Wheels/Tires:	13x5J/165HR-13
Units Produced:	38,703 (1971-75), 5,783 (2002tii Touring 1971-74)
Maximum speed (kph/mph):	190/118
Notes:	In 1973, North American versions received impact bumpers and side-clearance lights. The tii was not available in the US after 1974. Touring versions had 5-speed manual, larger gas tanks and other specifications similar to 2002tii.

North American late tii had extended bumpers, which unfortunately added length and weight to a rapidly slowing sports model. (Author photo)

The tii steering wheel and dash were identical to the "cooking" models except a clock was included. (Author photo)

Late-model 2002 rear view illustrates safety bumper, ample trunk access and BMW owner humor with regard to custom license plate. (Author photo)

Here's the 02 Touring. From the side, the 1802, 2002 and 2002tii were identical. Although the Touring design was smart and practical, it never caught on with BMW buyers. There hasn't been a BMW hatchback since the last of the Tourings in 1974. Slotted steel wheels marked later cars. (BMW Werkfoto)

Tourist plates attached, this 1972-74 2002tii was ready for a European tour before being shipped to the US. US car had side-marker lights, bumper guards and different license plate lighting. (BMW Werkfoto)

Typical action at a BMWCCA meet. This 2002's heeled over and being driven with brio. (BMWCCA photo courtesy Yale Rachlin)

The 1502 was sold in Europe only. This "oil crisis" econobox was a good seller and lasted until 1977—two years after the new 3-Series was introduced. Low-compression, 75 bhp engine ran on regular gas; car lacked some trim but represented good value. (BMW Werkfoto)

2002TI was distinguished by its grille badge. This twin-Solex-carbed 120 bhp variant did not appear (officially) in North America. (BMW Werkfoto)

Closeup of the 2002TI powerplant. The injection tii was more suitable for the US emissions regulations. (BMW Werkfoto)

CHAPTER 9
Turbo
1973-1974

BMW pioneered extensive use of turbocharging back in 1972: first, with an experimental gullwing sports coupe (which visitors can see today in the BMW museum) and, later, in the factory speedster, the 2002 turbo of 1973-74.

The Turbo show car, primarily a design exercise, previewed the exciting looks of the later M1, and used a 200 bhp 2002tii four (mounted transversely amidships) with a side-mounted standard four-speed 2002 transmission.

The car's gullwing doors opened into a very contemporary, space-styled cockpit with deep buckets, a tiny, businesslike leather wheel and broad horizontal instrumentation.

From a styling point of view, the Turbo's dramatically shaped hood bulge, which extended back from the futuristic twin kidney grilles, would greatly influence the next generation of passenger cars. The modified engine exponent continued in a very special, limited-production version of the 2002, the 2002 turbo.

Beginning with a standard 2002tii, BMW engineers added a KKK compressor mated to a new intake manifold. Boost pressure was relief valved at 8 psi. The compression ratio was dropped from the tii's 9.5:1 to a more tractable 6.9:1. Most of the other engine components remained unaltered, including the Kugelfischer mechanical fuel injection.

An optional five-speed gearbox linked to the revised 170 bhp motor yielded eight-second 0-60 times and a top end of 125 mph. Full boost took effect at 3800 rpm and the turbo's rear axle ratio was changed from the tii's 3.64 to 3.36.

While faster than any Series 02 car, the turbo was still slower than some of BMW's "fast freight" sedans. The car's complicated turbo system was trouble prone and the mirror-image turbo lettering on the air dam made it hard for adults to take this car seriously (it was later removed). Pricing, was only 4,000DM more than a ti, but was soon increased another 2,000DM—still substantially less than the 6-Series coupes.

Only 1,672 turbos were made over a two-year period and none were officially exported to the US, as the factory did not move to attain the proper certification. It's said reliably that the turbo was "cleaner" than the certified tii.

Calling the turbo, "the most desirable BMW this side of the 507," Georg Kacher, writing in *Car* magazine, talked about his Turbo impressions a few years ago:

"The BMW 2002 turbo was a Janus-faced car. Up to 4,000 rpm it was very similar to the tii. The steering was perhaps a trifle heavier, the handling perhaps not quite as sharp, a change influenced by the extra weight under the bonnet and by the wide 6.0 x 13 wheels fitted with fat 185/70 VR tires. Past the 4,000 rpm mark, however, the turbo suddenly turned into a different car. As if someone had switched on a second engine, the blower cut in with all its thrust, pushing the car ahead at an incredible speed, still going strong when the needle hit the lifesaving 6500rpm ignition cut-out.

"Although the powerplant delivered its goods with great smoothness and surprising mechanical refinement, the complete change of character that occurs the moment you hit 4,000 rpm made the blown BMW a brutal car to master on the road, a beauty turned beast and vice versa."

Turbo drivers quickly learned that, under hard acceleration, in wet conditions or through a turn, the sudden onslaught of power over 4,000 revs could cause the little cars to

Designed as an "experimental safety vehicle," the fiberglass BMW Turbo of 1972 was a forerunner of the production M1. Energy-absorbing front and rear bumper systems telescoped under impact. Gullwing doors incorporating side-impact bars, a wide roll bar and a radar warning device that signaled the driver when other cars were too close—these Turbo features were highly touted in 1972 when Munich built two prototypes. (BMW Werk-foto)

get sideways really easily—and quick, opposite lock to correct (not to mention a cool head) was necessary.

Still, if you're a 2002 fan, this car is the ultimate and those few cars that have made it to the US are reverently worshipped at BMW gatherings. (Presently in Germany, BMW builds another factory Turbo, the 745i, and we'll discuss this long-legged sedan in the 7-Series section.)

For my money, and for better performance, while the turbo is a fascinating anomaly, I'd recommend you spend your used BMW budget on a 6-Series coupe.

<table>
<tr><td colspan="2" align="center">BMW Turbo</td></tr>
<tr><td colspan="2">Engine</td></tr>
<tr><td>Type:</td><td>in-line, water-cooled 4</td></tr>
<tr><td>Bore x Stroke (mm):</td><td>89x80</td></tr>
<tr><td>Displacement (cc):</td><td>1990</td></tr>
<tr><td>Valve Operation:</td><td>sohc</td></tr>
<tr><td>Compression Ratio:</td><td>6.9:1</td></tr>
<tr><td>Carburetion:</td><td>Kugelfischer mechanical fuel injection and KKK turbocharger</td></tr>
<tr><td>BHP (mfr DIN):</td><td>200@6000</td></tr>
<tr><td colspan="2">Chassis and Drivetrain</td></tr>
<tr><td>Transmission:</td><td>4-speed manual</td></tr>
<tr><td>Steering:</td><td>rack & pinion</td></tr>
<tr><td>Front Suspension:</td><td>MacPherson struts, torsion bars</td></tr>
<tr><td>Rear Suspension:</td><td>double lateral links, lower trailing links, torsion bars</td></tr>
<tr><td>Axle Ratio:</td><td>n/a</td></tr>
<tr><td colspan="2">General</td></tr>
<tr><td>Wheelbase (mm/in):</td><td>2400/94.5</td></tr>
<tr><td>Track front/rear (mm/in):</td><td>1550/1530-61.0/60.2</td></tr>
<tr><td>Brakes:</td><td>disc/disc</td></tr>
<tr><td>Wheels/Tires:</td><td>14x9½J/4.75/11.2-14</td></tr>
<tr><td>Units Produced:</td><td>2 (1972)</td></tr>
<tr><td>Maximum speed (kph/mph):</td><td>250/155</td></tr>
<tr><td colspan="2">Notes: An experimental fiberglass-bodied mid-engine sports coupe, the Turbo was a 1972 forerunner of the M1 and the production 2002 Turbo. A built-in electronic device signaled the driver if the car was too close to the car ahead. Impact bumpers, a roll bar and side-impact door bars added to the Turbo's safety potential.</td></tr>
</table>

<table>
<tr><td colspan="2" align="center">2002 Turbo</td></tr>
<tr><td colspan="2">Engine</td></tr>
<tr><td>Type:</td><td>in-line, water-cooled 4</td></tr>
<tr><td>Bore x Stroke (mm):</td><td>89x80</td></tr>
<tr><td>Displacement (cc):</td><td>1990</td></tr>
<tr><td>Valve Operation:</td><td>sohc</td></tr>
<tr><td>Compression Ratio:</td><td>6.9:1</td></tr>
<tr><td>Carburetion:</td><td>Kugelfischer mechanical fuel injection and KKK turbocharger</td></tr>
<tr><td>BHP (mfr DIN):</td><td>170@5800</td></tr>
<tr><td colspan="2">Chassis and Drivetrain</td></tr>
<tr><td>Transmission:</td><td>4- or 5-speed manual</td></tr>
<tr><td>Steering:</td><td>worm & roller</td></tr>
<tr><td>Front Suspension:</td><td>MacPherson struts, coil springs, antiroll bar</td></tr>
<tr><td>Rear Suspension:</td><td>semitrailing arms, coil springs, anti-roll bar</td></tr>
<tr><td>Axle Ratio:</td><td>3.36</td></tr>
<tr><td colspan="2">General</td></tr>
<tr><td>Wheelbase (mm/in):</td><td>2500/98.4</td></tr>
<tr><td>Track front/rear (mm/in):</td><td>1375/1362-54.1/53.6</td></tr>
<tr><td>Brakes:</td><td>disc/drum</td></tr>
<tr><td>Wheels/Tires:</td><td>13x5½ or 13x6/185-70 HR-13</td></tr>
<tr><td>Units Produced:</td><td>1,672 (1973-74)</td></tr>
<tr><td>Maximum speed (kph/mph):</td><td>210/130</td></tr>
<tr><td colspan="2">Notes: Turbo fuel tanks had 5.3 gallons more fuel than standard 2002's. Options included alloy wheels and the 5-speed transmission. The "reverse-scripted" front spoiler did not last long after criticism arose. Gas shocks and lowered ride height were optional.</td></tr>
</table>

For its time, the Turbo's futuristic interior was a sensation—with aircraft-like instrumentation surrounds, deep buckets and a heavily padded steering column. The Turbo's transversely mounted 200 bhp four had a side-mounted four-speed attached. (BMW Werkfoto)

According to the factory, the 2002 turbo was "... designed for chiefly sporty persons." The lettering on the front spoiler was soon abandoned as buyers found it annoying. (BMW Werkfoto)

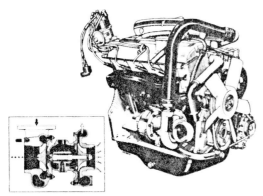

KKK compressor at 8 psi provided the turbo's urge. A Kugelfischer injection system (like the tii's) ensured plenty of fuel when the boost was called up. (BMW Munich drawing)

Extended fender flares, wide wheels, lowered suspension and Motorsport striping were all turbo trademarks. (BMW Werkfoto)

Fat, purposeful wheel and added instruments in the middle of the dash distinguished the 2002 turbo. (BMW Werkfoto)

In contrast with a 2002, the turbo was lower, meaner, quicker and more functional. Side lights were an owner addition, along with telescoping bumpers, to certify this Turbo for US registration. (John A. Bergen photo)

CHAPTER 10
The Glas BMW

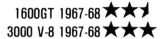

1600GT 1967-68 ★★✈
3000 V-8 1967-68 ★★★

As BMW's renaissance continued, the resurgence in manufacturing demanded more and more space. BMW looked around for expansion possibilities and found a company whose misfortunes it had shared short years before. Hans Glas Gmbh, in the city of Dingolfing, ninety miles from Munich, was slowly dying. The Glas werkes had built a strange range of cars, beginning with the patently absurd Goggomobil minicar, but stretching into interesting territory with the Glas 1700GT fastback and an even more ambitious effort, the Glas 3000V8.

The situation by mid-1966 was this: BMW needed a car factory in a hurry and Glas was terminal. Munich bought out Glas and, for one year, manufactured the two top-of-the-line Glas efforts as stopgap BMW's. But more BMW parts than just badges were involved: A revised Glas 1700GT, now called the BMW 1600GT, was built from September 1967 to the following August. There were 1,259 of these coupes made, equipped with BMW engines, rear suspensions and twin-kidney grilles. While the GT's would top 115 and a convertible variation showed promise, they still weren't BMW's, and factory plans for the 3-Series (to be made at Dingolfing) superseded any chance they might have had.

The other Glas-BMW effort involved a Frua-bodied, three-liter, V-8-powered coupe that picked up the nickname Glaserati. Its styling seemed to be borrowed from the Italian roadburner. The three-carburetor, cogged belt-driven sohc V-8 developed 160 bhp and powered the car to a true 121 mph top end. As BMW had its own coupe plans in the works, the BMW Glas 3000's days were numbered; it was ignominiously dropped in September 1968.

You have to be a real dyed-in-the-wool Bimmerphile to even want a Glas BMW, although the 1600's appear in the US from time to time and they're really not bad cars. Parts? Forget it in terms of sheet metal, but as the 1600 shared a number of stock BMW components, there's hope for you. While the rarity of the 3000 V-8 models (only 389 were built) is undeniable, I don't recommend them as high-buck collector cars. The 3000 suffers from its short wheelbase, both in terms of looks and handling, but if you're determined to have one of everything in your BMW collection, happy hunting!

BMW Glas 1600 GT

Engine
Type: .... in-line, water-cooled 4
Bore x Stroke (mm): 84x71
Displacement (cc): 1573
Valve Operation: .... sohc
Compression Ratio: 9.5:1
Carburetion: .... twin Solex 40 PHH
BHP (mfr DIN): .... 105@6000

Chassis and Drivetrain
Transmission: .... 4- or 5-speed manual
Steering: .... worm & roller

Front Suspension: .... independent A-arms, coil springs, antiroll bar
Rear Suspension: .... semitrailing arms, coil springs
Axle Ratio: 3.64

General
Wheelbase (mm/in): 2320/91.3
Track front/rear (mm/in): 1260/1260-49.6/49.6
Brakes: .... disc/drum
Wheels/Tires: 4½J-14/155HR-14
Units Produced: 1,259 (1967-68)
Maximum speed (kph/mph): 185/115
Notes: Some sources say 1,255 produced.

This plucky Goggomobil was never destined for the BMW roundel, but its bigger brothers became Bimmers for a while. (BMWCCA photo)

With its BMW 1600TI engine, the Glas coupe was a brisk performer. Sadly, sales failed to reach expectations. (BMW photo)

The Glaserati, a Frua-designed V-8 coupe, lasted just a year before being dropped in 1968. BMW needed manufacturing space in Dingolfing to build its new 2500 Series. (Yale Rachlin photo)

BMW's 3000 was a fast, attractive car, but less than 400 were sold. With the 2800CS on the way, the two models would have been in conflict even if Munich hadn't needed the manufacturing space. (BMW photo courtesy Richard O. Neville)

BMW Glas 3000 V-8

Engine

Type:. . . . . .90° water-cooled V-8
Bore x Stroke (mm): 78x78
Displacement (cc): 2982
Valve Operation:. . . . . sohc
Compression Ratio: 9.2:1
Carburetion: . . . .3 Solex 35 DDIS (later cars had two Solex)
BHP (mfr DIN): . . . . .160@5100

Chassis and Drivetrain

Transmission:. . . . . 4-speed manual
Steering: . . . . .power-assisted worm & roller
Front Suspension: . . . . independent A-arms, coil springs,
  antiroll bar
Rear Suspension:. . . . . . .DeDion axle, three half-leaf springs
  Panhard rod
Axle Ratio:. 3.364

General

Wheelbase (mm/in): 2500/98.4
Track front/rear (mm/in): 1432/1412-56.4/55.6
Brakes:. . . . . disc/disc
Wheels/Tires: . . . . .5½JK-14/185H-14 or 185HR-14
Units Produced: 389 (1967-68)
Maximum speed (kph/mph): 195/121
Notes: Some sources say 277 produced.

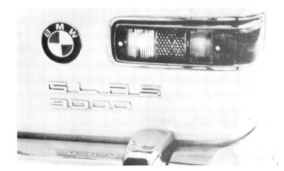

BMW-Glas 3000 was a handsome car from all angles. To put punch behind promise, there was 160 hp and a 200 kph top end. (BMW photo courtesy Richard O. Neville)

CHAPTER 11
The New Sixes

2500	1968-77	★ ★
2800	1968-77	★ ★
3.0S	1971-77	★ ★ ★
Bavaria	1971-77	★ ★ ★
2.8L	1974-77	★ ★
3.0L	1974-77	★ ★ ★
3.3L	1974-77	★ ★ ★

By mid-1968, following the success of its smaller cars, it was high time for BMW to build a serious, medium-price-range, four-door sedan. The 501/502 Series had faded away in 1964 (hopelessly outdated) without an advanced replacement. Now, with sales on an upswing, BMW could return to active pursuit of Mercedes-Benz—and the engineers and designers went after their Stuttgart rivals with an impressive new entry.

Alexander Von Falkenhausen's freshly designed six-cylinder led the way. A close look at this new engine clearly evidences its evolution from the chain-driven sohc fours. Offset thirty degrees, with an aluminum head and seven main bearings, the classy powerplant came in two variations: a 170 bhp 2500 and a 192 bhp 2800. Both engines had an 86 mm bore; the strokes were 71.6 mm and 81.0 mm, respectively. The new trispherical, turbulence bowl combustion chamber (called Dreikugelwirbelwannenbrennraum in the wonderful way the German language stacks adjectives) design successfully permitted a high power output along with compliance with the ever-stricter US emissions regulations. Fuel consumption was tolerable and results were achieved without the dreaded air pumps and exhaust gas recirculators.

Twin dual-throat Zeniths provided the carburetion. The oversized cylinder block had plenty of room to grow—and grow it would over the next few years.

BMW had done its homework, with combinations of features that set new standards for the class. Although the 2500/2800 suspension system was a variation of the four-cylinder models, the front MacPherson struts were angled rearward. This allowed more effective bump compliance and contributed to an antidive effect under braking. Any adverse steering effects from this arrangement were effectively canceled by optional power steering. In back, the coil springs for the trailing arms were repositioned.

Braking was handled by power-assisted four-wheel discs and the system incorporated dual hydraulic circuitry (the extra circuit operated calipers on one side of the front brakes while the primary system operated the second side of front calipers and the rear brakes). The parking brake was handled Porsche-style with a small drum built into the rear discs.

The 2500 model provided an attractive entry price and was somewhat a bare-bones approach. The 2800 was much more luxurious. Standard equipment included an antiroll bar for the rear suspension, Boge Nivomat self-leveling struts in the rear and an electric rear window defroster. Luxury touches such as oversized tires, a built-in tool kit in the trunk and an upgraded level of interior trim were 1,765DM extra. An automatic transmission, a ZF three-speed, was a 1,332DM premium for both models.

The cars were well received by the American automotive press, but prices (well into the mid-$5,000 range) were a little high. For that money, you could have had a new XKE!

The new 2500 presented attractive styling and quality appearance that would evolve, with tasteful modifications, into a basic look for a decade. (BMW Werkfoto)

In North America, Max Hoffman cleverly marketed the 2500 with a 2800 engine for $5000, and the Bavaria was born. (Mark Borkowski photo courtesy BMW Senior Six Register)

Here's what *Road & Track* roadtesters thought of the 2500/2800: "The all-new six-cylinder engine is a jewel. At low speeds, it combines a sporting exhaust note with a modest amount of BMW cam-drive whine and practically no other underhood noise; as the revs climb toward its redline of 6200 rpm, it takes on a snarl delightfully like that of a Porsche 911 . . . In through-the-gears acceleration, the 2500 is as impressive to the clocks as it is to the ear, producing quarter-mile times that any self-respecting Detroit engineer would say can't be done with 2.5 liters, 3,000 pounds and tractability. And, like all BMW's, the 2500 is designed to run all day at its maximum speed which turns out to be 118 mph."

Road & Track criticized the 2500's optional power steering and its tendency toward inside wheel lifting on hard corners, concluding: "It costs a lot, but that's the price you pay for top quality, and there is no doubt that its performance is faster, more sporting and longer-legged than that of its nearest competitor."

Sensing that the pricing was a restriction, Max Hoffman convinced the factory to produce an interesting amalgam of BMW trim and performance. The 1971 New York Auto Show launched the Bavaria—basically a 2800 with less luxurious trim, and the self-leveling suspension was also no longer available. This judicious paring brought the Bavaria's price in at a very acceptable $4,987. Interestingly, however, few basic Bavarias were ordered, either by dealers or customers so a "loaded" Bavaria packing power steering, tinted glass, air conditioning, the deluxe radio and so on saw the tag quickly climb over $6,000.

The Bavaria's new price positioning accomplished BMW's purpose and sales steadily increased. Predictably, the 1971 Bavaria was called by *Road & Track* "one of the world's great buys in luxury sedans."

The 2500 was discontinued in North America but it was sold in Europe through 1977. The 2800, now imported as the Bavaria to the US, was also produced through 1977 and a long-wheelbase version, the 2.8L was available only in Europe from 1975-77. The 2.8L's basic engine and suspension details were identical to the shorter-wheelbase car but the wheelbase, track and overall length were all changed for the stretched version. The 2.8L's price was about 3,500DM more than its smaller sister.

Continuing the Bavaria's momentum, the car received a big-bore three-liter increase in 1972—home-country 2800's had received this boost the previous year. The European version was a 180 bhp stormer. Sadly, due to US emissions modifications ten horsepower were dropped. In Germany, the new car was called 3.0S. It was quickly followed by a Bosch D-Jetronic injected version, the 3.0Si, with 200 bhp (DIN) at a relatively low 5500 rpm. In 1975, the German buyer could also choose a long-wheelbase version of the three-liter car, the 3.0L. This car was the recipient of a carbureted 3.3 liter overbore, and the inevitable injection model 3.3Li option was a choice for two years, 1976-77. Interestingly, the higher-horsepower fuel-injected version had a two-millimeter stroke decrease (it was actually a 3.2-liter) but in keeping with a practice dropped only recently, BMW kept the larger-displacement name.

The American 3.0Si, which became available in late 1976, saw a 200 bhp powerplant for the first time, continuing BMW's reputation for performance. *Road & Track* made the inevitable comparison of a carbureted three-liter Bavaria to the then-current Jaguar XJ6 and Mercedes-Benz 280 sedans. The editors criticized BMW's cold-weather start performance, and suggested that Bavaria buyers spring for the rear antiroll bar which was now an extra-cost option. During this period, BMW changed its roll-bar policy frequently (as it would later do on the 3-Series). A best bet for the older cars: Be sure to install roll bars front *and* rear for top performance.

BMW topped its competition in engine performance, automatic transmission (the early ZF's were not up to the standard of the later Borg-Warner Model 65 three-speed), instrumentation and controls. The testers criticized the 3.0's ride, noise level and styling but

Dash of the 2800 showed clearly visible instruments grouped in front of driver. Bucket seats and floor shift underscored that this sedan, while luxurious, was still a performer. (BMW Werkfoto)

2500	
Engine	
Type:.............................	in-line, water-cooled 6
Bore x Stroke (mm):	86x71
Displacement (cc):...............................	2494
Valve Operation:................................	sohc
Compression Ratio:.............................	9.0:1
Carburetion:	twin Zenith 35/40 INAT
BHP (mfr DIN):	150@6000
Chassis and Drivetrain	
Transmission:........	4-speed manual or 3-speed automatic
Steering:	worm & roller (power assist optional)
Front Suspension: .... MacPherson struts, coil springs, antiroll bar optional until 1971, standard thereafter	
Rear Suspension:......semitrailing arms, coil springs, antiroll bar standard until 1971, then optional	
Axle Ratio:....................................	3.64
General	
Wheelbase (mm/in):	2692/106.0
Track front/rear (mm/in):	1446/1464-59.9/57.6
Brakes:......................................	disc/disc
Wheels/Tires:	14x6J, 175HR-14
Units Produced: ..93.363 (1968-77), some sources say 94.026	
Maximum speed (kph/mph):	190/118
Notes: BMW's new big 6 was a real Mercedes contender. This successful engine design was marked by automatic transmission problems in its early years. Standard equipment on 2500's included a lavish tool kit, which would become a BMW hallmark. After 1971, the 2500 was not available in North America.	

Companion model 2800 had 20 bhp more. Limited-slip differential and self-leveling rear suspension were standard equipment in the beginning but deleted in 1971. (BMW Werkfoto)

concluded, ". . . look at the Bavaria's price; nearly $1,500 below the comparably equipped Mercedes and even more below the Jaguar . . . the Bavaria is simply a sensationally good buy at either its base price or loaded with extras."

The big sedans, in standard (US and Germany) and long-wheelbase (Europe only) variations were all phased out in 1977 when the 7-Series cars became the top-of-the-line offerings.

For a limited time, in the UK, a 3.0 Si Estate wagon was built by Langley Motors of Thames Ditton, Ltd. and distributed through BMW dealers. The roof was extended in station wagon fashion and a rear hatchback allowed six feet of usable rear flat space. Extras included a fabric sun roof, tow bar, roof rack and even a dog guard. One was recently offered for sale in a British publication for less than £2,000—a very rare car indeed.

For the collector market, the Bavaria and its cousins, the earlier 2500/2800 and the later 3.0Si, are fast tourers. Their drawbacks lie in repair expense, and the difficulty of obtaining spare parts. If you're really looking for good and reliable transportation, a "bargain" price on a Bavaria might be tempting, but you can get a lot more value for your money with the early 5-Series and later 7-Series cars.

2800/Bavaria, 2.8L

Engine
Type:. . . . . in-line, water-cooled 6
Bore x Stroke (mm): 86x80
Displacement (cc): 2788
Valve Operation: . . . . sohc
Compression Ratio: 9.0:1
Carburetion: . . . . twin Zenith 35/40 INAT
BHP (mfr DIN): . . . . 170@6000

Chassis and Drivetrain
Transmission:. . . . . . . .4-speed manual or 3-speed automatic
Steering: . . . . worm & roller (power assist optional)
Front Suspension: . . . . MacPherson struts, coil springs, antiroll bar optional until 1971, then standard
Rear Suspension:. . . . . .semitrailing arms, coil springs, antiroll bar standard until 1971, then optional
Axle Ratio:. . . . . 3.45, 3.64 (L)

General
Wheelbase (mm/in): . . . . 2692/106.0, 2792/109.9 (L)
Track front/rear (mm/in): . . . . . . .1446/1464-56.9/57.8, 1480/1486-59.2/59.4 (L)
Brakes:. . . . . disc/disc
Wheels/Tires:. 14x6J/195/70HR-14
Units Produced: . . . . 39,056 (1968-74), 5,036 (1975-77 L)
Maximum speed (kph/mph): . . . . 200/124, 195/121 (L)
Notes: 2.8L was not the first long-wheelbase sedan variant. The first was the 1973 3.3L. Most Bavarias were fitted with air conditioning. Bavaria name plates found their way onto many other makes. Self-leveling rear suspension was deleted at the end of 1971.

3.0S/Bavaria, 3.0Si, 3.0L

Engine
Type:. . . . . in-line, water-cooled 6
Bore x Stroke (mm): 89x80
Displacement (cc): 2985
Valve Operation:. . . . . sohc
Compression Ratio: . . . . 9.1:1, 9.5:1 (after 9/76, 9.0:1), 9.1:1 (Si), 8.3:1 (Bavaria)
Carburetion: . . . . . twin Zenith 35/40 INAT, Bosch L-Jetronic (Si)*
BHP (mfr DIN/SAE):. . . . .180@6000 (US, Bavaria 170@5800), 200@5500 (176@5500) (Si)

Chassis and Drivetrain
Transmission:. . . . . . . .4-speed manual or 3-speed automatic
Steering: . . . . worm & roller (power assist optional)
Front Suspension: . . . . MacPherson struts, coil springs, antiroll bar
Rear Suspension: . . . . semitrailing arms, coil springs, optional antiroll bar
Axle Ratio:. 3.45

General
Wheelbase (mm/in): . . . 2692/106.0 (S, Si), 2792/109.9 (3.0L)
Track front/rear (mm/in): 1446/1464-56.9/57.6
Brakes:. . . . . disc/disc
Wheels/Tires:. . . . . 14x6/195/70HR-14 (US: 175HR-14), 195/70VR-14 (Si)
Units Produced: . . . . 32,567 (1971-77), 20,310 (1971-77)**
Maximum speed (kph/mph): . . . . 205/127, 210/130 (Si), 200/124 (L)
Notes: 3.0L wheelbase (introduced 1975) was 2792 mm/109.9 inches. US 3.0Si was always equipped with Bosch injection. European cars received fuel injection beginning in September 1976. The first US 3.0S appeared in 1974, three years after the model was introduced. 5,521 3.0L's were produced 1975-77.
* D-Jetronic injection until September 1976, replaced by L-Jetronic
** 3.0L units produced, 5,521; 3.0S, 51,544

Bavaria nameplate found its way onto a lot of other German cars although the model was marketed this way only in North America. This Bavaria has correct chromed nameplate, custom exhaust, terrific license plate. (Author photo)

The '72 Bavaria dash is still contemporary; steering wheel is an accessory, so are seat covers. (Author photo)

This 1972 US Bavaria sports late-model accessory mirror, optional full hubcaps. Watch out for rust on the early cars. Replacing fenders on this Bavaria could be expensive. (Author photo)

Extended bumpers weren't bad from dead astern. Metal panel behind license plate was no longer painted to match body color. (Author photo)

Not too tidy but still powerful, Bavaria 2800 engine cleaned a lot of clocks in its day. (Author photo)

Later Bavarias (1974) had the dreaded US bumpers. (Author photo)

2.8L and 3.0L shared identical body. The 3.9-inch-longer wheel-base allowed more room in the rear. (BMW Werkfoto)

North American 3.0S incorporated modernized styling, those awful bumpers again and alloy wheels that would be seen on the entire range before long. (BMW Werkfoto)

3.3L/3.3Li

Engine
Type:................................. in-line, water-cooled 6
Bore x Stroke (mm):.................... 89x88.4, 89x86 (Li)
Displacement (cc):........................3295, 3210 (Li)
Valve Operation:................................. sohc
Compression Ratio:.............................. 9.1:1
Carburetion:........ twin Zenith 35/40, Bosch L-Jetronic (Li)
BHP (mfr DIN):.................. 190@5500, 197@5500 (Li)

Chassis and Drivetrain
Transmission:........4-speed manual or 3-speed automatic
Steering:.................. power-assisted worm & roller
Front Suspension:........ MacPherson struts, coil springs,
  antiroll bar
Rear Suspension:.......... semitrailing arms, coil springs
Axle Ratio:... 3.45

General
Wheelbase (mm/in):..................... 2792/109.9
Track front/rear (mm/in):............ 1480/1486-58.3/58.5
Brakes:................................... disc/disc
Wheels/Tires:..................... 14x6J/195/70VR-14
Units Produced:...3,022 (1974-77), some sources say 3.3L =
  1,622 and 3.3Li = 1,401 for a total of 3,023
Maximum speed (kph/mph):....................205/127
Notes: When fuel injection appeared, the engine was de-
  stroked 2 mm, but the 3.3 designation remained.
  Automatic transmission was standard, but the 4-speed
  gearbox was available on request.

European 3.0S had squared Teutonic styling, "regular" bumpers, abundance of chrome trim. (BMW Werkfoto)

European 3.0Si with decorative Bavarian maiden. The 200 bhp fuel-injected engine gave this car a 130 mph top end; not bad for a luxury sedan. (BMW Werkfoto)

Last of the line, the European 3.3Li had 3210 cc engine, 197 bhp
with Bosch L-Jetronic injection. The 109.9-inch wheelbase was
the same as on early L models. (BMW Werkfoto)

1974 North American 3.0Si had the usual protection differences.
Longer bumpers made the car look top-heavy, almost clumsy.
(BMW NA photo)

2000C 1965-69	★★★	
2000CS 1965-69	★★★✦	
2.5CS 1974-75	★★★	
2800CS 1968-71	★★★✦	
3.0CS 1971-75	★★★✦	
3.0CSL 1971-72	★★★★✦	
3.0CSi 1971-75	★★★★	
3.0CSL 1972-73	★★★★✦	
3.0CSL 1973-75	★★★★★	

With the 2000 sedans an assured success, by June 1965, BMW turned its attention to a sports coupe once again. The beginning was nearly the end. BMW stylists designed a 2+2 and Karosserie Karmann in Osnabrück began building the bodies.

From a rearview styling perspective, the 2000C coupe was lovely. Up front, the design had to be called awkward at best. The bluff, rounded nose with flush grilles and wraparound lights looked somehow unfinished. But the overall correctness of the design carried the day. Typically, the engineering staff was already hard at work preparing hotter engine options.

The "cooking version" 2000C had a 100 bhp four with a single Solex carburetor. To slow it even further, a three-speed ZF automatic was optional. The hot version, called 2000CS, had a 120 bhp, twin-Solex two-liter four and came only with a four-speed manual gearbox. With the CS, a clear, new BMW direction was established and the company's growing following could look for the coupes to set Munich's performance standards.

The 2000CS used the 2000TI's engine and a higher rear axle ratio to send it winging along at 115 (versus the 2000C's 104 mph top end). While it still wasn't an autobahn winner the coupe's handling was quite acceptable. Despite its unfortunate nose, the car attracted buyers and lingered on until the late summer of 1968. Its replacement confirmed BMW had a sense of styling to go with its renewed performance image.

The coupe body, from the windshield posts back, anyway, had a feeling of timeless grace, so stylists knew where to concentrate their efforts. The 2800CS bowed with the powerful new 165 bhp (DIN) 2800 six in a slightly stretched (75 mm longer) chassis to accommodate the bigger powerplant. The new coupes had a wider track and wheels than their predecessors but, curiously, did not immediately get the sedan's four-wheel disc brakes. The redesigned sedan front suspension was included and the pattern was set for BMW coupes for a long time to come.

At last, the 503 and 507 were avenged with the aggressive, purposeful 2800CS. The big six easily claimed the title of BMW's quickest (128 mph) and most luxurious car to date. The redesigned front end was bold and fast-looking, in keeping with the car's ability to blow off nearly everything in its lane. Pricing, at just under 23,000DM (a lot less than its luxo-coupe predecessors) was acceptable in Germany but less so in the US where at $8,100 the car competed head-on with Jaguar ($6,250), Mercedes 2505L ($7,654) and Porsche ($7,995).

The motoring writers tripped over one another with praise for the new coupe. Writing in *Wheels,* Jerry Sloniger called the car "Velvet-Gloved Dynamite." Said Sloniger: "This coupe makes the most ham-footed driver among us look like Fangio setting lap records on his least frenetic day."

Road & Track confirmed the feelings: "Putting the 2788cc 192-bhp (SAE) six into this car has resulted in all the expected performance improvements plus a new standard of sophistication and understated luxury for 6-cylinder cars. . . . The big BMW engine . . . is without

2000C/2000CS

Engine

Type: .... in-line, water-cooled 4
Bore x Stroke (mm): 89x80
Displacement (cc): 1990
Valve Operation: .... sohc
Compression Ratio: .... 8.5:1, 9.3:1 (CS)
Carburetion: .... one Solex 40 PDSI, twin Solex 40 PHH (CS)
BHP (mfr DIN): .... 100@5500, 120@5500 (CS)

Chassis and Drivetrain

Transmission: .... 4-speed manual or 3-speed automatic,
  4-speed manual (CS)
Steering: .... worm & roller
Front Suspension: .... MacPherson struts, coil springs*
Rear Suspension: .... semitrailing arms, coil springs*
Axle Ratio: .... 4.11, 3.90 (CS)

General

Wheelbase (mm/in): 2550/100.4
Track front/rear (mm/in): 1330/1376-52.4/54.2
Brakes: .... disc/drum
Wheels/Tires: ......14x5½J/6.95/1755-14, 6.95/175S-14 (CS)
Units Produced: .... 2,837 C, 1965-69, 8,883 CS, (1965-69)
  Some sources say 9,999 (CS) and 3,692 (C)
Maximum speed (kph/mph): .... 168/104, 185/115 (CS)
Notes: The coupe weighed 65 lbs more than its sedan counter-
  part. *Antiroll bar was optional on C and standard on
  CS.

Oh that front end! The 2000's bizarre snout and curious headlamps were unattractive, but the rest of the design showed promise. (Author photo)

2000CS had an additional 20 bhp from twin Solex carburetors. Although the coupe weighed slightly more than the 2000 sedan, performance and handling were acceptable. (BMW Werkfoto)

a doubt the most efficient and sophisticated in-line six in the world . . . Almost soundlessly willing at part throttle, it has the most beautifully subdued snarl when opened up . . . Handling is very good in all conditions, not as phenomenal as a Porsche 911 but exceptional for a luxurious 4-passenger car . . . Passengers are rarely aware of the level at which the driver is pressing on . . . there is nothing remotely approaching the 2800CS for significantly less . . . so anyone with $9,000 or so to spend must find the 2800CS close to irresistible."

In April 1971, BMW upped the ante with a bored-out (89 mm versus 86 mm) version of the 2800CS called the 3.0CS. With 180 bhp (DIN) on tap in Germany (ten fewer horsepower in the US version), the addition of rear-wheel disc brakes and a new four-speed Getrag gearbox, the BMW coupe had firmly established its place among the world's best grand tourers. A new Borg-Warner automatic replaced the ZF automatic.

American cars had the federally mandated side running lights, a lower compression ratio and altered tuning for emissions and leather upholstery as standard equipment (it was optional in Europe).

Motor correspondents drove the new 3.0CS and noted there was very little difference in top speed compared with the 2800CS due to a rev limiter which took effect at 6200 rpm. They found that the new model was half a second quicker accelerating to sixty than its predecessor and was able to reach 100 from a standing start a significant two seconds faster than the 2800CS could manage. Interestingly, however, they were critical of the coupe's handling: "We still don't think this hybrid coupe (an amalgam of the big BMW saloon running gear and ex-2000 coupe shell) matches some of the lesser BMW saloons on handling, good though it undoubtedly is. On normal roads it feels taut, precise and predictable but bumpy, twisty roads induce some diagonal pitching, and lifting the throttle in mid-corner can make the car feel a bit twitchy." The testers criticized the big steering wheel which they felt added resistance and made it difficult to steer the car smoothly.

On the other hand, *Autocar*'s John Bolster had nothing but praise for the 3.0CS handling: ". . . the wider light-alloy wheels and tires, plus the new steering geometry, continue to give a higher ultimate cornering speed than previous models could encompass."

In the fall of 1971, Bosch electronic fuel injection made its appearance. With it, a 9.5:1 compression ratio and adjustments to valve timing, the willing six pumped out 200 bhp (DIN) at 5500 rpm and the car became the 3.0CSI. Although carbureted cars were still available, the lure of a 137 mph top speed brought buyers forward even though the "spritzer" versions cost another 3,000DM.

With this type of performance on tap, and more lurking just beneath the surface, it was only a matter of time before BMW could (and did) go racing. The factory prepared a number of CS coupes for Group 2 sedan racing—with predictable success.

In order to compete evenly with the then-winning V-6 Capris, BMW developed a lightweight coupe. The need for homologation spawned a BMW classic: the 3.0CSL. The L was for leicht (light), just as in the SSKL Mercedes of the thirties. Karmann continued to make the bodies, but in the CSL's case, the car's aluminum doors, hood and trunk saved over 300 pounds. The CSL was a very distinctive car sporting tailfins and a rear wing developed to handle the car's high top speed. Street versions of the CSL added 5,000DM to the price tag.

Over the course of its exciting life span, the CSL went from a carbureted 180 bhp three-liter to a 200 bhp injected engine; then a 0.25 mm bore increase followed (for 3003 cc). Next, the 89.25 bore version received a 4 mm stroke increase for 3153 cc and 206 bhp. Factory racing CSL's used even more exotic engines: four-valve heads, 3.5 liter displacements, sky-high compression ratios and outrageous cam variations yielding outputs in excess of 430 bhp. Needless to say, the street CSL's are very highly prized and for the racing cars, be prepared to write a big, big check, indeed.

Comfortable, functional cockpit of the 2800CS. (Author photo)

The new grille was a big improvement over the bulbous and clumsy 2000. Fog lights were an owner-added accessory. (Author photo)

2800CS posed proudly for its factory picture. With 170 bhp and a nine-second 0-60 time, these quick coupes corrected the 2000's styling problems and offered substantially more performance. The six-cylinder coupe legend was about to begin. (BMW Werkfoto)

Interestingly, when the OPEC fiasco began in 1973, imposition of strict speed limits in Germany forced BMW to take a retrograde step in the accelerated development of its super-coupes. A CS appeared with the sedan's "cooking" 150 bhp 2.5 liter engine. At 28,500DM, buyers sacrificed a little performance (the car would still top 200 kph) and saved 3,000DM over the three-liter cars. A few other spartan touches, such as steel disc wheels, fixed rear quarter windows and unassisted steering kept prices down until the Arabs took the heat off.

While the later 6-Series coupes are lovely, most BMW enthusiasts prefer the earlier 2800CS, 3.0CS and 3.0CSI, with the 3.0CSL as the all-time desirable coupe. If you're looking for a coupe there are more than a few caveats, however. These cars were never really rust-proofed very well from the factory and they can rust through where the front MacPherson struts mount to the upper bodywork. Unfortunately, the box frame members actually form a sort of "mud trap," and spray from the wheels can reach the fuse box. Geoff Howard, writing in *Thoroughbred & Classic Cars*, pointed out a few of the big six's shortcomings:

"At the rear, the fuel tank and its mountings are . . . vulnerable which makes a potential safety hazard. . . . the aluminum boot, bonnet and doors of the CSL are frighteningly expensive." Howard suggests replacing damaged alloy panels with steel parts. I'd caution against that as it will have a detrimental effect on the car's value.

The coupe's ventilated front discs are crack prone if used hard; rear springs tend to settle after some high mileage and the gearbox synchro rings will weaken over time. Most of the aforementioned problems are accented with abuse, so it pays to know something about the type of driver (and mileage) your prospective purchase has endured. Coupe body and engine parts are expensive for any model, and spares for the earlier 2800's are becoming harder to locate.

These coupes still have the performance measure of their later cousins—at a lot less money. A well-maintained or restored coupe attracts a good deal of admiration in BMW circles and the accelerating prices indicate it won't be long before these cars attain serious pricing levels.

2800CS

Engine
Type:. . . . . in-line, water-cooled 6
Bore x Stroke (mm):. 86/80
Displacement (cc):. 2788
Valve Operation:. . . . . sohc
Compression Ratio:. 9.1:1
Carburetion: . . . . twin Zenith 35/40 INAT
BHP (mfr DIN):. . . . . .170@6000

Chassis and Drivetrain
Transmission:. . . . . . . .4-speed manual or 3-speed automatic
Steering: . . . . .power-assisted worm & roller
Front Suspension: . . . . MacPherson struts, coil springs, antiroll bar
Rear Suspension:. . . . . semitrailing arms, coil springs, antiroll bar
Axle Ratio:. 3.45

General
Wheelbase (mm/in): 2625/103.3
Track front/rear (mm/in): 1446/1402-56.9/55.2
Brakes:. . . . . .front disc, rear drum
Wheels/Tires: . . . . 14x6J/175HR or 195/70HR-14
Units Produced: 9,399 (1968-71)
Maximum speed (kph/mph):. 206/128
Notes: The 2800CS retained the 2000CS rear section, with a more attractive frontal design. Although 2800 sedans had 4-wheel discs, curiously, the 2800CS retention of the 2000 C axle left it with drum brakes. Only 1,167 coupes were exported to the US.

2.5CS

Engine
Type:. . . . . in-line, water-cooled 6
Bore x Stroke (mm):. 86x71.6
Displacement (cc):. 2494
Valve Operation:. . . . . sohc
Compression Ratio:. 9.1:1
Carburetion: . . . . twin Zenith 32/40 INAT
BHP (mfr DIN):. . . . . .150@6000

Chassis and Drivetrain
Transmission:. . . . . . . .4-speed manual or 3-speed automatic
Steering: . . . . worm & roller (power assist optional)
Front Suspension: . . . . .MacPherson struts, coil springs
Rear Suspension:. . . . . semitrailing arms, coil springs
Axle Ratio:. 3.64

General
Wheelbase (mm/in): 2625/103.3
Track front/rear (mm/in): 1446/1398-56.9/55.0
Brakes:. . . . . .disc/disc
Wheels/Tires: 14x6J/175HR-14
Units Produced: 844 (1974-77)
Maximum speed (kph/mph):. 200/124
Notes: The 2.5 was a fuel-crisis, economy alternative to the 3.0CS. By reverting to disc wheels, unassisted steering, fixed windows, reduced trim, the price of this smaller-engined car was substantially reduced. The 2.5 was not offered in North America.

Coupe's trim rear is set off by wraparound bumpers, back-up lighting integrated into rear molding and discreet exhaust. The 2800CS used 2000CS suspension and rear drums. Wider wheels increased the new model's track by an inch. (Author photo)

Smart alloy wheels set off new coupe look. (Author photo)

Rear view of a 2800CS automatic. Script on the rear and minor cockpit differences identified the automatic cars. Three-speed automatic used small floor lever in center console. (Author photo)

2.5CS was factory's fuel-crisis fighter. Despite reduced trim, plain wheels and reduced power, the "economy" coupes (sold in Europe only) would still top 124 mph. (BMW Werkfoto)

Lovely 3.0 at a BMWCCA concours featured accessory mirrors and lights. Sleek lines looked best in a dark color. (Author photo)

This '72 CS without the side lights and reflectors is a much sought-after car among BMW aficionados. (Author photo)

View of a Weber-carbureted 3.0 (left). Weber carbs are a popular modification. The stock Zenith-carbureted 3.0 (right) and its air cleaner for comparison. (Author photo)

3.0CS and CSi were identical save rear identification script. New alloys hid ventilated discs now fitted at all four corners. This 3.0CS automatic was North America bound. Note safety bumpers, marker lights and tow hook. (BMW Werkfoto)

Another North American 3.0CS. BMW elected not to change a good thing. Evolutionary coupe changes improved handling, braking and acceleration. This '73 CS escaped the bumper regs which plagued '74 cars. (BMW Werkfoto)

The CSi had no visible differences from the CS save identification, but the additional 20 bhp from the Bosch D-Jetronic injection was noticeable in the upper rev ranges. (Author photo)

Deep, cradling buckets in the CSL meant business; padded wheel gave a good grip at car's top end of 138 mph. (BMW Werkfoto)

The 3.0CSL used a lot of aerodynamic tricks. These cars had many varied engine and carburetion combinations but, no matter what's under the hood, these lightweights are highly desirable. (BMW Werkfoto)

From the rear, the 3.0CSL was equally unusual. Window spoiler and rear wing kept the light rear stable at high speeds, certainly attracted attention, too. (BMW Werkfoto)

3.0CS

Engine
Type:............................. in-line, water-cooled 6
Bore x Stroke (mm):.............................. 89x80
Displacement (cc):................................2985
Valve Operation:................................... sohc
Compression Ratio:............................... 9.1:1
Carburetion: ....twin Zenith 35/40 INAT
BHP (mfr DIN/SAE):.................180@6000/170@5800
Chassis and Drivetrain
Transmission:........4-speed manual or 3-speed automatic
Steering: ....power-assisted worm & roller
Front Suspension: .... MacPherson struts, coil springs,
  antiroll bar
Rear Suspension:......semitrailing arms, coil springs, anti-
  roll bar
Axle Ratio:.. 3.45
General
Wheelbase (mm/in): 2625/103.3
Track front/rear (mm/in): 1446/1402-56.9/55.2
Brakes:... disc/disc
Wheels/Tires:.....................14x6J/195/70VR-14
Units Produced: .... 11.063 (1971-75), some sources say
  10.088
Maximum speed (kph/mph): 213/132
Notes: In April 1971, the coupe received rear disc brakes.

3.0CSi

Engine
Type:............................. in-line, water-cooled 6
Bore x Stroke (mm):.............................. 89x80
Displacement (cc):................................2985
Valve Operation:................................... sohc
Compression Ratio:............................... 9.5:1
Carburetion: .... Bosch D-Jetronic fuel injection
BHP (mfr DIN):.............................200@5500
Chassis and Drivetrain
Transmission:........4-speed manual or 3-speed automatic
Steering: ....power-assisted worm & roller
Front Suspension: .... MacPherson struts, coil springs,
  antiroll bar
Rear Suspension:......... semitrailing arms, coil springs,
  antiroll bar
Axle Ratio:.. 3.25
General
Wheelbase (mm/in): 2625/103.3
Track front/rear (mm/in): 1971-72, 1446/1402-56.9/55.2
  1972-73, 1426/1422-56.1/55.9
  1973-75, 1470/1426-57.8/56.1
Brakes:... disc/disc
Wheels/Tires:.....................14x6J/195/70VR-14
Units Produced: .....8.199 (1971-75), some sources say 8.142
Maximum speed (kph/mph): 220/136

Injected CSi engine was impressive. (Author photo)

Twin-Solex 2000CS developed 120 bhp. Coupe's decent handling made up for a lack of power—all was corrected when the sixes bowed. (BMW Werkfoto)

Here's the ultimate: a CSL in racing trim with widened wheels and fenders, front air dam and single windscreen wiper. Stripes indicate this was a works CSL. Note brake cooling vents in the air dam. (Gary Gold and Yale Rachlin photo)

3.0CSL

Engine
Type:. . . . . in-line. water-cooled 6
Bore x Stroke (mm): 1971-72 89x80. 1972-73 89.25x80. 1973-75 89.25x84
Displacement (cc): . 1971-72 2985. 1972-73 3003. 1973-75 3153
Valve Operation:. . . . . sohc
Compression Ratio : 9.5:1
Carburetion: . . . . . . .1971-72 twin Zenith 35/40 INAT. 1972-75 Bosch D-Jetronic fuel injection
BHP (mfr DIN): . . . . . . .1971-72 200@5500. 1973-75 206@5600

Chassis and Drivetrain
Steering: . . . . worm & roller (power assist optional)
Front Suspension: . . . . MacPherson struts. coil springs. gas inserts. antiroll bar

Rear Suspension: . . . . . . semitrailing arms. coil springs. gas inserts. antiroll bar
Axle Ratio:. 3.25

General
Transmission:. . . . . 4-speed manual
Wheelbase (mm/in): 2625/103.3
Track front/rear (mm/in): 1971-72. 1446/1402-56.9/55.2
1972-73. 1426/1422-56.1/55.9
1973-75. 1470/1426-57.8/56.1
Brakes:. . . . . disc/disc
Wheels/Tires: 14x7J/195/70VR-14
Units Produced: . . . .1.039 (1971-75). some sources say 1.096
Maximum speed (kph/mph): . . . . . . .dependent upon gearing (140+ mph is possible)

CSi/CS comparison show stock alloys versus popular BBS accessories, sidelights on '73 car are obtrusive compared to '72 in European trim. (Author photo)

Roundels everywhere identified the six-cylinder coupe. (Author photo)

Reclining front buckets and deep rear seats made 2800CS a true 2+2. (Author photo)

With the New York skyline in the background, the first of BMW's super coupes makes quite a statement. (BMW Werkfoto)

These coupes *can* autocross. Some body lean is evident but the CS coupes take it in stride. (BMWCCA *Roundel* photo courtesy Yale Rachlin)

320i 1975-77 ★★
320i 1977-81 ★★⚬
320i 1981-83 ★★⚬

With the success of the 2002 and BMW's establishment of a definite niche with its sporty little sedans, a distinct market trend began. Characteristically, Munich was never wont to sit on its laurels.

The new 3-Series bowed in early 1975 to mixed reviews among Bimmer aficionados. Nearly everything went up—price, weight, size, insulation—except a key factor, acceleration. The new car was a definite improvement over its predecessors, but the lean, sporty characteristics which had endeared the more spartan 2002's to a performance-oriented market, were "engineered" out.

Ironically, in a pattern that has continued for BMW to this day, sales increased. Many customers chose BMW for its reputation. They didn't have to prove anything on a twisty stretch of road. Loyalists vowed to keep their 2002's forever. They insisted the factory had "gone soft," and the controversy still continues.

The 320i styling is credited to Paul Bracq, who also did the striking BMW Turbo. While unmistakably BMW, the new car was an early recipient of the now-fashionable wedge shape. The cockpit, with its wraparound instrument panel, was a welcomed scaled-down version of this feature on the bigger Bimmers. The aircraft-derived, softly glowing orange instrument lights were very visible, reassuring and professional.

The lines of the US 320 are spoiled somewhat by the dreaded 5 mph bumpers. Shorter, less-protective but better-looking European bumpers harmonized with the car's lines more effectively. The massive bumpers, plus extra insulation accounted for the US car tipping the scales at 150 pounds more than the European version.

Bigger (5.5-inch) rims, usually smartly styled alloys with 185SR-13 Continentals, Michelins or Pirelli P-3's, round out the specification.

Many of the 320i engineering improvements—split fuel tanks under the rear seat, inclined MacPherson strut independent front suspension, an adaptation of the traditional BMW trailing arm independent rear suspension, and slower but more precise rack-and-pinion steering—showed careful attention to detail. However, there were some inherent negatives, too.

A chronic steering wobble appeared—unfortunately, at the critical 55-60 mph speed range. This malady is incurable no matter how carefully you check the alignment, balance the wheels and select true tires. The factory conveniently looks the other way on this one. Many enterprising Bimmer buffs have solved this annoying feature with an antishimmy modification consisting of two flat plastic spacers which often ends the problem (however, this doesn't always work and requires well-balanced wheels).

Coupled with the new suspension's smoothness is another unwanted 3-Series quirk: a tendency toward trailing throttle oversteering. The 320i is a handler, all right, but it's not forgiving past a certain rate of knots. Again, there's a fix: Bilstein or Koni shocks, the thicker rear sway bar from the Sport package (omitted after 1977) to reduce trailing throttle oversteer and some performance tires (Stahlflex 3011's or P-6 Pirelli's) magically transform the car.

Under the hood, the former two-liter four was destroked to 1.8 liters in 1979. While unfettered European 320's developed 125 bhp, their American cousins made do with a slightly

Plain disc wheel was standard—most North American buyers opted for the finned alloys. (Author photo)

While purists decried the 320i, the new car was an improvement over the 2002 in many ways but remained slower than the 2002tii. Destroked to a 1.8 liter in 1979, the North American 320 got slower while its European counterpart retained muscle and even added a six. Pre-1980 320i's had mirrors mounted on door sides (chromed) while later cars had first one, then two, integrated, flat-black mirrors. (BMW NA photo)

strangled 110 bhp—and with the weight increase caused by the creature comfort improvements, the cars were noticeably slower.

The Bosch K-Jetronic fuel injection is another contrast, compared with the race-bred Kugelfischer plunger-pump injection system. The old fuel injection was designed for speed, the new system is an economy and emissions compromise.

Over the years, BMW embarked upon a systematic weight reduction program for the 320. At the same time, recognizing the popularity of certain add-on upgrades, the company also made available an optional Sport package featuring a sunroof, sport wheels, Recaro seats, a three-spoke steering wheel and a stiffer suspension.

The 320 remains a smooth performer, but a lot of the old urge is gone. Still, in the fuel-conscious US, 0-60 in twelve seconds and a true top of 110 were reasonable figures for most of the 320's life span. It was enough for "the car that started a cult."

320/320i (Europe, USA)

Engine
Type:.......................... in-line, water-cooled 4
Bore x Stroke (mm): ....89x80, 89x71 (i)
Displacement (cc): ....1990, 1766 (i)
Valve Operation:.................................... sohc
Compression Ratio:........ 8.0:1, 9.3:1 (320i), 8.8:1 (US 320i)
Carburetion: one Solex 32/32 DIDTA, Bosch K-Jetronic (320i)
BHP (mfr DIN/SAE):....109@6000, 125@5700/110@5800, US after 1981 102@5800

Chassis and Drivetrain
Transmission:............. 4- or 5-speed manual or 3-speed automatic
Steering: ....rack & pinion, power optional
Front Suspension: .... MacPherson struts, coil springs, antiroll bar
Rear Suspension:......semitrailing arms, coil springs, antiroll bar
Axle Ratio:....................................3.64

General
Wheelbase (mm/in): 2563/100.9
Track front/rear (mm/in): 1364/1377-53.7/54.2 (320), 1386/1399-54.6/55.1 (320i)
Brakes:..................................... disc/drum
Wheels/Tires: 13x5J/165SR-13 (320), 13x5½J/185/70HR-13 (320i)
Units Produced: .... 1975-77 (320 replaced in Europe by 320-6) 1977-83 (320i production in US)*
Maximum speed (kph/mph): .... 170/105 (320), 180/112 (320i Europe), 169/105 (320i US)
*For 3-Series unit production, refer to 320/6, 323i.

Frontal aspect of 320i features 5 mph bumpers, fog lamps below. Original license plate mounting on bumper made it vulnerable to careless parkers. A simple mount dropped the plate safely below the bumper. (Author photo)

320i rear was cleanly defined. This 1980 car has a fixed passenger-side mirror, sport (nonfactory) exhaust, optional alloy wheels and a popular handling improver for 320's: Phoenix 3011 Stahlflex tires. (Author photo)

Sport option rear deck was devoid of identification. (Author photo)

Plucky 1.8 liter four was no match for the old 2002tii, despite updated injection. Most buyers didn't seem to mind. (Author photo)

BBS wheels, sport exhaust and other subtle modifications mark
this 320i. Striping was often a dealer-added option. (Author photo)

Top up or down, the Coach Builders, Ltd., Inc., 320i convertible
conversion is a car the factory should have built. (Courtesy Larry
McCann)

Contemporary US BMW racer showed what a little development could do for the right design. Aerodynamics played a key role in the car's changes—IMSA race series has seen successful 320's battling a wide range of competitive GT's. (BMWCCA photo courtesy Yale Rachlin)

Sport package air dam was functional. Note correct front license bracket. (Author photo)

Sport wheels were by Lemmer. Although suspension was improved, engine was not modified. (Author photo)

320 1975-77 ★★
320-6 1983- ★★
323i 1983- ★★★
316 1983- ★★
318 1983- ★★
315 1983- ★★

The 3-Series has four distinct variants in Europe and none of them are marketed (through BMW dealers, anyway) in the US. The car is available for a low price in much of Europe and the UK with a 90 bhp 1573 cc four or a 98 bhp 1766 cc four. While inexpensive and spartanly trimmed, these cars will still top 100 mph and do it all day in relative comfort. I know, I rented a Hertz 318 and drove from Munich to Brussels in one day flat out. The European 318 felt little slower than my US 320 and, except for a few missing niceties, represented quite a bargain. It's a car BMW enthusiasts would love to see in the US but the low profit margin, import limitations and tight competition from Japan understandably result in the company trying to sell more luxuriously equipped cars.

The smaller displacement European 3-Series cars are a bit confusing. BMW sold a 316 from 1975-80. From 1980, the 316 badge was on a 1.8 liter car and the 1.6 liter car had a 315 badge.

320's in Europe are 1990 cc fours. A 109 bhp version was sold from 1975-77 and it was superseded by the 125 bhp 320i, the car American 320 owners wish they had. From 1977 onward, German buyers could also opt for the 320-6, a 122 bhp two-liter six that featured BMW's delightful little M60 six-cylinder powerplant. The hotrod in this European series remains the 2.3 liter 323i. Fitted with Bosch K-Jetronic fuel injection, the 323i is a minirocket that is the first 3-Series car that aficionados compare on the same basis as the lost 2002tii.

The 323i—with its split exhausts and 120 mph top end—is a sprightly little car and a number of gray marketers have adapted it for sale in the US. It comes equipped with four-wheel disc brakes to go with its 143 bhp speed capability, and a front grille badge that is usually seen close up in the rearview mirror of any autobahn dawdlers!

The new 3-Series was launched in Europe in mid-1975 with the 320 model in two flavors: carbureted and Bosch injected. The grille badge and integrated bumpers were characteristic of European cars. (BMW Werkfoto)

316 variant provided a low-buck 3-Series alternative. Rear badges, plain wheels, single headlights were identification clues. (BMW Werkfoto)

320-6/323i

Engine
Type:.............................. in-line, water-cooled 6
Bore x Stroke (mm): 80x66
Displacement (cc): 1990
Valve Operation:................................. sohc
Compression Ratio: 9.2:1
Carburetion: .... Solex 4Al, Bosch K-Jetronic (323i)
BHP (mfr DIN): .... 122@6000, 143@6000 (323i)
Chassis and Drivetrain
Transmission: ...4- or 5-speed manual or 3-speed automatic
Steering: ....rack & pinion, power optional
Front Suspension: .... MacPherson struts, coil springs, antiroll bar
Rear Suspension: ......semitrailing arms, coil springs, antiroll bar
Axle Ratio (s):.................................... 3.64
General
Wheelbase (mm/in): 2563/100.9
Track front/rear (mm/in): 1386/1399-54.6/55.1
Brakes: .... disc/drum, disc/disc (323i)
Wheels/Tires: 13x5½J/185/70HR-13
Units Produced: .... Factory data does not distinguish between model and calendar year for current BMW models. 1978-82 3-Series production worldwide was 1,001,521.
Maximum speed (kph/mph): 183/113, 192/119 (323i)

320-6 was supplanted by injected 323i powerplant. Although a tight fit in a 3-Series, the bored-
out six is a real Q-ship. (Author photo)

European 318 was forerunner of second-series North American
320i powerplant. The carbureted 98 bhp four represented a good
value. (BMW Werkfoto)

The Baur cabriolet, never officially imported into North America, was an attractive compromise between coupe and convertible. The integrated roll bar provided protection, while the open-air feature let in the sun. (Courtesy Karosserie Baur GmbH, Stuttgart)

When you see this face in your rearview mirror, pull over! 323i drivers have an aggressive autobahn reputation—sparked by the 143 bhp, 120+ mph capability of this little rocket. (BMW Werkfoto)

When the European 3-Series was launched, its four-cylinder engine received changes introduced earlier in North America—the tri-spherical combustion chambers, two-barrel Solex and low-compression motor allowed use of regular gasoline. This is the 1800 engine. (BMW Werkfoto)

316/318 (Europe)

Engine

Type:	in-line, water-cooled 4
Bore x Stroke (mm):	84x71, 89x71 (318)
Displacement (cc):	1573, 1766 (318)
Valve Operation:	sohc
Compression Ratio:	8.3:1, 9.5:1 (318)
Carburetion:	one Solex 32/32DIDTA
BHP (mfr DIN):	90@6000, 98@5800 (318)

Chassis and Drivetrain

Transmission:	4- or 5-speed manual, 4- or 5-speed manual or 3-speed automatic (318)
Steering:	rack & pinion
Front Suspension:	MacPherson struts, coil springs, antiroll bar
Rear Suspension:	semitrailing arms, coil springs, anti-roll bar
Axle Ratio:	4.11, 3.90 (318)

General

Wheelbase (mm/in):	2563/100.9
Track front/rear (mm/in):	1364/1377-53.7/54.2
Brakes:	disc/drum
Wheels/Tires:	13x5J/165SR-13
Units Produced:	1975-83; redesigned in 1983
Maximum speed (kph/mph):	161/100, 168/104 (318)

Notes: Easily recognized by dual headlamps, this model is continued in the rebodied 3-Series. A great entry-level European BMW.

There are many minor differences in this series, consult chart on page 154, **BMW, The Complete Story**, by W. Oswald, for complete details.

Racing 3-Series cars is big business in Europe. In the mid-seventies, BMW commissioned artists Frank Stella, Alexander Caldwell and Roy Lichtenstein to custom paint its racers. Here is a 320i by Roy Lichtenstein. This coupe ran at the 1977 Le Mans classic. (BMWCCA *Roundel* photo courtesy Yale Rachlin)

CHAPTER 15
The "New" 3-Series

315 (E 1983-) ★★
316 (E 1983-) ★★
318i (US 1984-85, E 1983-) ★★★┛
320i (E 1983-) ★★★┛
323i (E 1983-85) ★★★★┛
325 (US 1986-) ★★★┛
325e (US 1984-) ★★★
325es (US 1986-) ★★★
325i (E 1985-) ★★★★┛
M3 (E 1986-) ★★★★
324d (E 1985-) ★★
325Xi (E 1985-) ★★★★┛

The long-awaited 3-Series revamp was both a joy and a disappointment to BMW enthusiasts. Typically, the Munich designers and engineers devoted their efforts to refinements, not radical changes. The styling was subtly changed, leaving the car tastefully but almost imperceptibly altered. The wedge shape was more pronounced, and BMW's very traditional look has been aerodynamically sculpted, with emphasis on curved front fenders, a deep air dam and a practical, if rather high, deck lid.

The old 1.8 liter sohc four soldiered on, developing the same 101 bhp, but a redesigned fuel-injection system provided a few extra pounds-feet of torque. The engine was smoother than the 320's, thanks to improved engine mounts and steering. BMW finally decided to combat its reputation for trailing throttle oversteer, and recognized a lot of aftermarket trends in the process. The new 318i rolled on smartly styled fourteen-inch alloy wheels with 195/60 high-performance Pirelli P6's. The front end was also revised: New sickle-shaped lower control arms in front and staggered shocks and springs in back noticeably improved handling.

Inside, the bucket seats were improved and they rolled forward to aid access to the back. The always fine dash was updated and the stereo repositioned.

Sadly, the new price of over $17,000, although it included a manual sunroof, alloy wheels and deluxe trim, took the 318i even further away from its traditional market. As an improvement over its predecessor, if you discount price for a moment, the 318i succeeded. But compared to contemporaries at far less money (like the Celica, Mazda 626 and so on) the BMW is overpriced, still slow and a bit old-fashioned in styling and appointments.

US Bimmerphiles, as this is written, have just received the high-performance 325e variant. It is a 323i-like rocket that has brought BMW's 3-Series reputation up to date once again. Cleverly, BMW elected to use the eta (efficiency) low-revving, high-torque six-cylinder 528e powerplant for the 325. It was already US certified and it combined good mileage with quick performance. As well, a four-door sedan, using both 318i and 325e powerplants, version was introduced in late 1984 (it was launched in Europe in the fall of 1983), and it should open a new portion of the market for BMW, not too late to underprice and outperform the baby Mercedes.

The new 3-Series coachwork came with a number of engine variants overseas. The car was available with 315, 316, 318 and 320 powerplants (as its predecessor was) and the 323i became the top-of-the-line once again. In this fashion, BMW was able to tailor its lower range for all markets, budgets and tastes. An M320i version was available in the US in early 1985 and announced for European release in late 1985. It incorporated many of the go-faster tricks from M-modified 5- and 6-Series cars. At the same time BMW planned to launch the 324td as the world's quickest diesel-powered passenger car. And in Europe, the long-awaited 325i was slated to replace the 323i.

Posed for an announcement picture, the new 3-Series clearly showed pinched grille, factory spoiler, wide P-6's. (BMW Werkfoto)

German 320i had sleeker side profile than first 3-Series, canted door posts, no side lights, new alloy wheel design, aero contours and rear-mounted antenna. (BMW Werkfoto)

For 1986, the big US 3-Series news involved the dropping of the 318i—the little four has been hard-pressed by competition. BMW NA replaced it with three versions of the six, the 325, 325e and 325es—all with ABS brakes as standard equipment.

While the US cars still made do with eta engines, European BMW fans received the 325i in a number of special configurations. The 2-door 325i remained the quickest 'standard' 3-Series variant, hotly pursued by a cabriolet version that received rave reviews at the Frankfurt show. With M-B's 190 clearly a winner, Munich countered with the droptop and a four-wheel-drive 325Xi, as well.

For high performance buffs, and to battle the 16-valve Mercedes 190, BMW developed the exciting M3, a twin cam four with updated aerodynamic styling, no-nonsense suspension and a close-ratio gearbox. Marginally quicker than the M-B 16-valve, the M3 was scheduled for European intro in late 1986, and plans to bring a federalized version to North America were set for the 1987 model year.

The BMW 324td didn't come but diesel fans could select the 324d, a normally-aspirated 2.4-liter oil burner that complimented the M-B 190D quite nicely. Britain's *Car* tested both competitors and felt the BMW 6 was superior to the Benz 5.

320 versus 318: Front-end taper, more integrated aerodynamics were evident. New 14-inch wheels were more functional, prettier than previous 13-inch alloys. (BMWCCA *Roundel* photo courtesy Yale Rachlin)

318's dash was subtly redesigned. Cockpit effect was more pronounced. Four-spoke steering wheel was comfortable. Note cruise-control stalk at right. (BMW Werkfoto)

Here I am, smiling after a 100-mph-plus dash through the San Antonio hills with the new 318i at the BMW press preview. Verdict: "The 318i's a big improvement over the 320i." (Author photo)

Viewed from behind, US 318 had squared trunk, impact bumpers and side lights. (BMW NA photo)

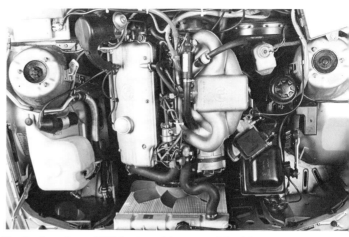

New sickle-shaped lower control arms improved handling and ride quality, and helped eliminate front-end shimmy common to the 320. (BMW NA photo)

North American 318i featured improved fuel injection. Improved engine mounts helped smooth the 1.8 liter four. (BMW NA photo)

318i (US)

Engine
Type:..................... in-line, water-cooled 4
Bore x Stroke (mm):.................. 89.0x71.0
Displacement (cc):......................... 1766
Valve Operation:............................. sohc
Compression Ratio:.......................... 9.3:1
Carburetion:................... Bosch L-Jetronic
BHP (mfr SAE):....................... 101@5800
Chassis and Drivetrain
Transmission:........5-speed manual or 3-speed automatic
Steering:.............. rack & pinion, power-assisted
Front Suspension:....... MacPherson struts, coil springs
Rear Suspension:......... semitrailing arms, coil springs
Axle Ratio:................. 3.64:1 (1984 3.91:1)
General
Wheelbase (mm/in):................... 2570/101.2
Track front/rear (mm/in):...... 1407/1415-55.4/55.7
Brakes:.................................. disc/drum
Wheels/Tires:............. 6Jx14-195/60HR-14
Units Produced:....... still in production 1983 to present
Maximum speed (kph/mph):.............. 180/111
Notes: Available in Europe in 315, 316, 320, 323i configurations. M325i will be available late 1984.

The 318i for the US featured smart alloy wheel styling shared with bigger Bimmers. These wheels are easier to clean than the old finned ones. (Author photo)

M3	
Engine	
Type:	in-line, water-cooled 4
Bore x Stroke (mm):	93.4x84
Displacement (cc):	2302
Valve Operation:	dohc 16-valve head
Compression Ratio:	9.6:1
Carburetion:	Bosch ML-Motronic fuel injection
BHP (mfr DIN/SAE):	200@6750
Chassis and Drivetrain	
Transmission:	5-speed manual
Steering:	power-assisted rack & pinion
Front Suspension:	independent, with double-joint control arm strut, coil springs, antiroll bar
Rear Suspension:	semitrailing arms, coil springs, antiroll bar
Axle Ratio:	4.23:1
General	
Wheelbase (mm/in):	2570/101
Track front/rear (mm/in):	1412/1434-55.6/56.4
Brakes:	disc/disc (ABS)
Wheels/Tires:	15x7J 205/55 VR 15
Units Produced:	(scheduled for late-1986 production in Europe, 1987 model year in US)
Maximum Speed (kph/mph):	ca. 238/146
Notes:	Bowing at the 1985/86 Frankfurt Motor Show.

European 323i had deep air dam with integrated fog lamps. Rear spoiler and twin exhaust marked the six-cylinder stormer. Note standard wheels—they're not available in North America. (BMW Werkfoto)

European 3-Series with the optional alloys. Recognizing popular aftermarket trends, BMW stole a march by offering attractive wheels, air dams and spoilers as factory accessories. (BMW Werkfoto)

323i and 318i (European) contrasted. The 323i trunk nameplate and spoiler were a subtle warning: Don't try to pass unless you've got something very quick. (BMW Werkfoto)

The popular BMW 3-Series was expanded from two to four models for 1985, available in either the familiar sporty two-door or the new, elegant four-door version. The 318i provided a durable, free-revving four-cylinder and the 325e has the refinement and power of six cylinders. (BMW NA photo)

325e interior sported deep bucket seats and new-design sports steering wheel as standard equipment. On-board computer was also a standard feature. (BMW NA photo)

The 325e bowed in April 1984 with 2.7 liter 121 bhp six shoehorned into the 318's engine bay. The eta engine provided lively performance with economy. (Courtesy BMW NA)

Close-up of new North American 3-Series instruments showing optimistic 140 mph speedo, mileage indicator, imprecise gas gauge compared to European liter indicator. (BMW NA photo)

325/325e/325es

Engine

Type:	in-line. water-cooled 6
Bore x Stroke (mm):	84.0x81.0
Displacement (cc):	2693
Valve Operation:	sohc
Compression Ratio:	9.0:1
Carburetion:	Bosch L-Jetronic
BHP (mfr SAE):	121@4250

Chassis and Drivetrain

Transmission: ....5-speed manual or 4-speed automatic
Steering: .... rack & pinion. power-assisted
Front Suspension: .... MacPherson struts. coil springs. antiroll bar
Rear Suspension: ......semitrailing arms. coil springs. anti-roll bar
Axle Ratio: 2.78:1

General

Wheelbase (mm/in): 2570/101.2
Track front/rear (mm/in): 1407/1415-55.4/55.7
Brakes: .... disc/disc
Wheels/Tires: 6Jx14-195/60HR-14
Units Produced: .... still in production 1984-to present
Maximum speed (kph/mph): 196/118
Notes: 325e marked the resurgence of BMW small car high-performance to the US markets. 4-door configuration was introduced in the US in the 1985 model year. The 3-Series for 1986 has ABS brakes standard. 325es has sport suspension.

Subtle differences marked US new 3-Series: Fog lights were standard, as were twin mirrors, new alloy wheels, impact bumpers and
side-marker lights. (BMW NA photo)

If you like sunshine, the soft-top 325i's for you.
This cabriolet is only available overseas at present but BMW NA is rushing it through EPA/DOT
work for 1987. Lines are very clean with the top
in place. I predict they'll sell like hotcakes; they're
already very popular in Europe.

Look closely, flared fenders and a side air dam
are the tip-off. Here's the 325 Xi, the four-wheel-
drive version of BMW's snappy 3-Series. Again,
North American enthusiasts have to be content
to dream about this one. Competition from Mercedes-Benz drove BMW's product planners to
offer them in a variety of modes—with top or
without, two or four doors, gas engine or diesel
and, lastly, two- or four-wheel drive.

And the best is yet to come. From the Motorsport Group, BMW's hot 3-Series variant, the M3, is the best little Bimmer yet. The four-valve 2302 cc twin cam takes BMW's venerable four to a new development high. The 200 bhp motor and up-rated suspension make the M3 a contender on road or track (this powerslide illustration indicates a bit of oversteer is still present, though). The M3 was introduced in Frankfurt in late 1985, but production wasn't scheduled for Europe until late 1986. Plans are to import the M3 into North America for the 1987 model year. (BMW Werk-foto)

325i

Engine
Type: . . . . in-line, water-cooled 6
Bore x Stroke (mm): 84x75
Displacement: 2494
Valve Operation: . . . . sohc
Compression Ratio: 9.7:1
Carburetion: . . . . .Bosch ME-Motronic fuel injection
BHP (mfr DIN/SAE): . . . . .126/171@5800

Chassis and Drivetrain
Transmission . . . . .5-speed manual (choice of 2 od or close-ratio sports) or 4-speed automatic (5-speed manual *only* on "all-road" four-wheel drive)
Steering: . . . . rack & pinion, power-assisted
Front Suspension: . . . . MacPherson struts, coil springs, antiroll bar
Rear Suspension: . . . . .semi-trailing arms, coil springs, antiroll bar
Axle Ratio: . . . . 3.4 or 3.91 (with sports gear box)

General
Wheelbase (mm/in): 2570/101.2
Track front/rear (mm/in): . . . . 1407/1415-55.4/55.7 (two-wheel drive),1420/1416-55.9/55.7 (four-wheel drive)
Brakes: . . . . disc/disc
Wheels/Tires: . . . . .5½J195/65 VR14 (two-wheel drive), 6J195/65 VR14 (four-wheel drive)
Units Produced: . . . . (currently under production)
Maximum Speed (kph/mph): . . . . .217/130 (two-wheel drive), 212/127 (four-wheel drive)
Notes: US enthusiasts have to be content (at this writing) with the eta-engined 325—in Europe, enthusiasts get the 323i's snappy successor, the 325i, in coupe, cabriolet and four-wheel-drive configurations.

In a sportier vein, the 325es two-door has the same engine as its lesser 3-Series brethren, but comes standard with a sport suspension, special front air dam, LSD, sport seats and performance M-Technic steering wheel. While the eta-engine still isn't a revver, the es handles nicely and is upholding BMW's performance image in the US until the M3 arrives.

CHAPTER 16
5-Series

518 1974-81 (E 1981-)	★★
520/520i 1972-77 (E 1977-81)	★★
525/525i 1973-81 (E 1983)	★★
530i 1974-77	★★★
528i 1978-81 (E 1981-)	★★★★
M535i (E 1979-80)	★★★★
528 (E 1975-77)	★★★
528e 1982-	★★★
524td 1985-	★★
535i (US 1985-)	★★★★
M535i (E 1985-)	★★★★
M5 (E 1985-)	★★★★★
518i (E 1984-)	★★
520i (E 1981-)	★★
525i (E 1983-)	★★
525e (E 1984-)	★★

E stands for Europe-only models

With the 02 models firmly established, BMW marketing, finally on track, began a new dimension of models which cleverly spanned and overlapped both its smaller and bigger cars.

The basis for the expansion in 1972 was the 520, a mid-sized sedan incorporating a new unit body and all-independent suspension. Initially, for Europe, two versions—a 115 bhp twin-carb four, the 520, and the 520i, an injected 130 bhp motor—were comparable to the 2002 and 2002tii.

The 2000 sedan was dropped and the new 5-Series, which was sized just under the company's six-cylinder cars, could be equipped, in time, with every one of the firm's powerplants. Michel Potheau believes the 5-Series received its designation because it was indeed the fifth new series after the V-8 Isetta era: 02, 2500/2800/Bavaria, CS, 3-Series and then the fives. A common belief is that the designation is an amalgam of passenger capacity and engine displacement.

Not unexpectedly in 1973, even though the 2500 remained in production, a new 525 with a 145 bhp six (versus the 2500's 150 bhp) was offered. The slight horsepower difference helped preserve some measure of dignity for the older model.

The versatility of the 5-Series platform allowed BMW to choose from a variety of powertrains in its line, then price and position the models according to trim, power and equipment variations.

In 1974, Munich simultaneously introduced its venerable 1800 cc four for Europe, Australia and other markets. In America, the three-liter sixes were featured, in both carbureted (530) and injected (530i) form.

As the 518 and 525 never made it to the US, we'll not spend time on them here. It would be nice to be able to similarly avoid the 530i, but one of the purposes here is to help you decide what to buy. Sadly, the 530i is not especially recommended.

BMW started out with the best of intentions: create a powerful medium-sized sedan expressly for the North American market. It was important to the factory folk that their new entry retain all the power of the 528 European cars, so they avoided de-smogging and reducing their existing powerplant. Instead BMW offered an overbored (98 versus 86 mm) 2985 cc six with Bosch L-Jetronic fuel injection (plans for the carbureted 530 were very short-lived due to the fuel injection's superiority).

The new 5-Series bowed in 1972 with carbureted and injected fours. These 520/520i's were not sold in North America. (BMW Werkfoto)

In 1973, the 525 appeared, followed two years later by the 528. These six-cylinder sedans continued the senior six tradition for BMW with 145 and 164 bhp, respectively, and top speeds over 120 mph. (BMW Werkfoto)

Designed to succeed the Bavaria, the 530i was the recipient of rave reviews at its American debut. *Road & Track* called the 530i one of its Ten Best Cars. With a 176 bhp engine coupled to a four-speed manual, topping 124 mph, there weren't many contemporary cars that could surpass it.

However, the compromises needed to meet EPA standards really choked the 530i's response at low speeds. BMW utilized a thermal reactor system which allowed the 530i to run on leaded fuel. Most of the other companies' solutions to the new regulations revolved around catalytic converters and unleaded gasoline. The BMW approach required a very rich mixture and a hot exhaust (achieved by retarding the spark at low speeds). These requirements as well as low-speed (up to 60 mph) throttle response murdered any hope of reasonable mileage.

In the beginning of the model's life, BMW offered it in a fifty-state version that struggled to achieve 12 mpg in the city and 15 mpg on the highway. Shortly afterward, a revised calibration was developed for forty-nine states; Californians were left with the worst of the 530i's. The "improved" model managed to average 19 mpg over a range of driving conditions.

But this was just the beginning of the 530i's problems: BMW sold 27,073 530i's in the US between 1975 and 1978. Slightly over eight percent of these cars suffered from cylinder head cracking problems. Michel Potheau feels the cracking problems arise from incorrectly torquing the cylinder heads, and from not retorquing them often enough.

BMW offered to repair the cars under its regular warranty program and there was (and may still be if you contact BMW North America) a goodwill program to repair cars which incurred the problem after the regular warranty period ended. As this is written, BMW will review any 530i cylinder-head problem; the company, pressed by a class action suit filed a few years ago, will generally help any owner with a legitimate claim. In 1980, BMW began to replace the original 530i heads with a new model casting that had a redesigned shape and 13 mm wide water jacket walls (the original walls were only 9 mm wide).

As if these problems weren't sufficient, 530i's have a few rust-prone areas, notably the rear wheel area on the passenger's side of the car. The rear wheel tends to displace dirt which is tossed against the gasoline tank; this can cause the tank and its surrounding area to corrode. Other rust problems involve the dogleg and, in some instances, rust can (and does) form where the side trim is attached.

The 530i also suffered from the heavier 5 mph "safety" bumpers. All in all, the first 530i's tested the patience of enthusiasts, but the same was true for all domestic and imported overseas products in those years.

BMW quickly got to work to improve the 530i: first, in the fuel economy department and, later, in 1977 with a whole series of changes. The 530i received a design facelift and the fuel-tank filter was moved from the rear of the car to the right rear quarter panel. Along with this change, the taillights were redesigned to be larger and more visible. A number of detail changes such as improved ventilation, increased sound insulation, electrically operated outside mirror and two-way sunroof improved passenger comfort while a change from solid to ventilated front disc brakes improved stopability.

The design change was especially evident from the front where the grille kidneys tapered straight back into a raised hood portion à la Turbo experimental car. This styling change was repeated later, in all the company's models, as was the development of an updated cockpit design featuring all the instruments and controls grouped handily around the driver for better ergonomics.

In 1978, the 530i received sportier, exposed wheels similar to a change that had already been seen on European models. The new wheels were standard equipment along with air conditioning, electric window lifts and power steering. BMW, like many manufacturers, was simply equipping the cars the way most of them were eventually ordered. This simplified manufacturing as fewer choices, except colors, were needed and dealers had cars everyone wanted.

With the fuel crisis dictating 1974's marketing strategy, BMW responded with the 90 bhp, four-cylinder 518. Trim rings were an extra-cost option, omitted here. (BMW Werkfoto)

520i/525i/525e

Engine

Type: . . . . in-line water-cooled 6
Bore x Stroke (mm): 80x66 (520i), 86x71.6 (525i)
Displacement (cc): 1990 (520i), 2494 (525i), 2693 (525e)
Valve Operation: . . . . sohc
Compression Ratio: 9.8:1 (520i), 9.6:1 (525i), 11.0 (525e)
Carburetion: . . . . . Bosch K-Jetronic (520i), Bosch L-Jetronic (525i)
BHP (mfr DIN): . . . . 125@5800 (520i), 150@5500 (525i) 177@3250 (525e)

Chassis and Drivetrain

Transmission: . . . . 4-speed manual or 3-speed automatic (5-speed manual available in the UK), 4-speed automatic (525e)
Steering: . . . . power-assisted worm & roller

Front Suspension: . . . . . . MacPherson struts, coil springs, antiroll bar
Rear Suspension: . . . . semitrailing arms, coil springs
Axle Ratio: 3.91 (520i), 3.45 (525i), 2.93 (525e)

General

Wheelbase (mm/in): 2625/103.3
Track front/rear (mm/in): 1430/1470-56.3/57.9
Brakes: . . . . disc/disc
Wheels/Tires: 14x5½J/175HR-14
Units Produced: . . . . Total 5-Series production worldwide from 1978-82 was 524.078 units
Maximum speed (kph/mph): . . 186/115 (520i), 197/122 (525i)
Notes: These cars were not available in North America. 525e has Bosch Motronic fuel injection.

The strength of the Mark against the dollar, along with all the added extras, saw prices soar to $14,800 on the East Coast, slightly higher on the West Coast.

In Europe, BMW also sold the twin carbureted 528 from 1975-77. In August 1977, the injected 528i was launched in Europe. Horsepower jumped from 165 to 176 due to the addition of a Bosch L-Jetronic induction system. Other changes from the 528 included new wheels—sans hubcaps or wheel covers—and some badge detail changes. European cars, of course, were still spared the 5 mph bumpers that BMW first introduced on the 530i for its bigger car series.

The following year, in keeping with what would become a consistent practice, BMW's 528i made its American appearance—probably to the intense relief of those enthusiasts who'd replaced their 530i cylinder heads. This time, Munich appeared to have the equation solved. The 528i displacement change came from a slightly reduced bore (86 mm versus 89 mm), but an advanced three-way catalytic converter and a Bosch Lambda sensor ensured the car lacked none of its predecessor's horsepower and punch, albeit on unleaded fuel this time.

The 528i met all the US federal and California emissions standards, beat the 530i fuel figures handily and was even faster (with an 8.2-second 0-60 clocking) than its predecessor. The price eased up over $15,000 but sales demand never wavered. With the 528i, BMW's reputation for high-performance sedans was unchallenged. The European version was good for 129 mph and even the heavier US car wasn't much slower.

In Europe only, in 1980 and 1981, BMW built a real pocket battleship in the 5-Series, the 218 bhp M-535i. The M denoted BMW's in-house racing division, BMW Motorsport. This 140 mph sportster is once again about to be offered, but if you can't wait, tuning firms will build you a facsimile—you just have to figure a way to certify it stateside.

For the US, with a growing interest in BMW but a markedly different climate in driving patterns and regulations, BMW was about to phase out the 528i in 1981 with a move that would surprise its dedicated fans.

BMW loyalists groaned when the factory announced a new car especially for the US in 1982. It was the 528e—e for eta (some said it was for "expensive")—and, compared on paper at first to the speedy 528i, it surely looked as though BMW had lost its sense of purpose.

The e-type's engine gave away 95 cc from the i and horsepower fell from 169 at 5500 rpm to 121 at 4250. The car's shocks, springs and suspension settings were a little softer, too. Under the hood, the revised six developed its peak torque, 170 pounds-feet, at 3250 rpm; versus the 528i's similar figure at 4500 rpm. The final drive ratio dropped from 3.45:1 to 2.93:1, again in keeping with an economy theme that was becoming apparent. Top speed dropped nearly 11 mph to 114.

Had BMW taken a major strategic turn away from its sporting image? Hardly likely. What the company did, taking into account US driving conditions compared to the wide-open German autobahns, was to build a fuel-efficient sporting sedan that conformed extremely well to its intended environment.

Of course, enthusiast magazines were horrified at first. *Road & Track* called the car "... a mixed blessing," but quickly became believers. "The big six enjoys being revved regardless of where the torque curve may be.... Interestingly enough, even though we were discouraged to see a BMW with slower acceleration numbers, the car doesn't feel slow. Thanks to the engine's impressive low and mid-range torque, the test track numbers we got for the 528e belie what you feel under your foot and your backside when driving it. In fact, the impression of power the 528e left was so strong, several of us were amazed to find it was even slower at all."

Car and Driver, too, had mixed emotions. "The 528e wrapped around the eta engine is definitely a low calorie car now ... A total of 1700 rpm has disappeared from the usable rev range which leaves the redline standing at a Cadillac-like 4700 rpm."

After driving the car for a while, however, *Car and Driver*'s editors made some prophetic comments: "It may just be that the 9000 or so doctors and lawyers and executives that will

For North America, BMW marketed the 530i with a 176 bhp engine and luxus trim. By 1975, all US cars had extended bumpers and side-marker lights. (BMW Werkfoto)

1977 530i showed new design features, raised hood profile and larger taillights. Two years later, BMW was still trading on *Road & Track*'s compliment that the 530i was the "best sedan in the world." (BMW NA photo)

buy 528e's next year will be happy with econothink. As it stands, the 528e is certainly worthy of its blue-and-white nameplate. But we can't shake the feeling that the difference between an excellent car and a spectacular one is as simple as bolting in last year's panzer powerplant."

The e's sales were double those of the 528i, which indicated that the market had clearly responded favorably to this sensible application of power and performance. I have (and *love*) a 1983 528e (having traded a 320i which my teenage sons outgrew). It's not a difficult car to enjoy; the e-type has been improved over three years with subtle styling detail changes, a slightly higher rev limit, new alloy wheels and so on. Compared with the competition (particularly the cramped new baby Mercedes with a similar price tag), the 528e offers more space and better performance (except for the Mercedes' slight edge in fuel economy). And it's a delightful car to drive.

533i

If you wanted a road rocket, the BMW lineup had one of those, too. When roadtesters at the 528e's preview pondered BMW's seeming disregard of its traditional, high-performance market, factory representatives promised a "hot" 5-Series car later in the production span. While some of the car magazines missed the call on a smart marketing decision that greatly broadened BMW's mid-range sales base, it didn't take a marketing genius to recognize that the new 533i, which bowed in early 1983, was the Bimmer they'd waited for. The new car's 3210 cc six packed 181 bhp at 6000 rpm and 195 pounds-feet of torque at 4000. The sedan weighed 200 pounds less than a 633CSi, so performance was back, in spades!

The 533i's Getrag five-speed had the same ratios as in the 528e. The rear-end ratio was 3.25:1 and top end, for the fastest production sedan in the country, was 134 mph. To go with all the performance, the factory added sport shocks and springs, improved Trac-Link semitrailing arm rear suspension, a padded steering wheel (optional on 528e's) and fat Michelin TRX tires on forged alloy 390x165 wheels.

The price tag was about $5,000 more than the 528e's and fuel mileage, understandably, gave away a few mpg to the economy version. With leather upholstery standard, the only two options available were a limited-slip rear (highly recommended) and an automatic transmission.

Roadtesters loved the new car, although the 533i's somewhat dated styling (compared with the jello-mold aero Audis and Fords) was criticized. Behind the wheel, editors were reminded what the car's intent was all about. Said *Road & Track*: ". . . the 533i is decidedly quick in any spectrum and goes about its motoring in exemplary fashion."

At *Car and Driver*, comments were similar. Csaba Csere said, "The 533i came just in time. I'd begun to despair that BMW would ever again build a rip-roaring sports sedan . . . [The 533i] shows that there is still a roaring performance fire burning deep inside BMW. Its engine is the kind that made the company famous—with its strong surge toward the revline, its silky smoothness and refinement—and the 533i is light enough to let it run freely."

With the 528e and 533i sharing the same basic configuration, BMW appealed to practical and sporting buyers simultaneously, with a car both types love.

524td

Another 5-Series variant—the 524td, a 2.4 liter turbo diesel—went on sale in the US in early 1985. Billed as the "fastest diesel sedan in the world," the td enjoyed earlier sales success in Europe. Its clever combination of diesel economy and BMW performance and handling is sure to give Mercedes marketers fits as the price (about $750 less than the 528e) considerably undercuts Mercedes-Benz' offerings.

BMW began td development when it looked as though a major portion of the market might go the oil-burner route. That hasn't happened, but the BMW diesel (which is also sold to Ford for use in the revamped Lincoln LSC Continental Mark VII) is bound to make believers out of folks who thought diesels had to be sluggish and noisy.

Using BMW's basic six as a pattern, the diesel is an all-new design with a cross-flow, swirl-chamber head and a Garrett T-3 Turbo set for an 11.6 psi boost. The DIN bhp rating is

An immaculate 530i at a BMWCCA meet; alloy wheels were a popular extra. Sadly, thermal reactor emissions control system on these cars led to cylinder head problems. (Author photo)

European 528i was aggressive. Michelin XWX's facilitated the car's 130 mph top end. (BMW Werk-foto)

518/518i

Engine

Type:.............................. in-line. water-cooled 4
Bore x Stroke (mm): 89x71
Displacement (cc):.................................. 1766
Valve Operation:...................................... sohc
Compression Ratio:....... 8.3:1; 9.0:1. Oct. 1980; 9.5:1, 1981
Carburetion: ..... one Solex 36-40 PDSI; Solex 32/32 DIDTA, Oct. 1980; Solex 2B4 1981-on
BHP (mfr DIN): ....90@5500/105@5500

Chassis and Drivetrain

Transmission:................. 5-speed or 4-speed manual
Steering: .... worm & roller
Front Suspension: .... MacPherson struts, coil springs. antiroll bar
Rear Suspension:.......... semitrailing arms. coil springs. optional antiroll bar
Axle Ratio:....................4.44; 4.27. Oct. 1980-present

General

Wheelbase (mm/in): 2536/103.0
Track front/rear (mm/in): 1406/1446-55.4/56.9
Brakes:..................................... disc/drum
Wheels/Tires:........................14x5½J/175HR-14
Units Produced: .... total 5-Series through December 31. 1978. was 467.112
Maximum speed (kph/mph): 163/101, 175/107
Notes: The 518 (still in production) was a fuel-saving addition to the BMW range in 1974. The 518 has never been available for sale in North America. L-Jetronic fuel injection.

115 at 4800 rpm and torque is 155 at 2400. The top end is 110 mph, with 5-Series handling standard equipment. Altogether, the td rounds out the BMW line and proves definitely that diesel drivers don't have to give up performance any longer.

535i

For 1985, BMW upped the ante again and the 533i became the 535i. BMW bored out the '33 and although horsepower was just up 1, to 182 bhp at 5400, the 3430 cc newcomer had nearly ten percent more torque. *Road & Track's* testers liked the new car. "There's no joking about the 535i's increased punch . . .," they wrote, ". . . The car wasn't hampered by our 533i's hop-skip routine off the line and it reached 30 mph a couple of tenths sooner; by 60, its edge had grown to 0.4 seconds. R&T found their 535i topped out at 131 mph, the previously tested 533i had a 134 mph top speed. "No matter," they said, "because either top end could get you in a whole pack of trouble almost anywhere in the world."

ABS brakes were standard, as befitting a sports sedan of this caliber, and there were some modest modifications to the seats to increase interior room. Although most of the car magazines decried the 5-Series' boxy, upright and rather dated styling, behind the wheel, there were few complaints.

The uprated 3.5-liter-engined 535i, closely following on the heels of the 533i, served notice to the competition that BMW was definitely back in the sport motoring game. The hot new powerplant, available in the 6- and 7-Series as well, underscored BMW's advertising with a real performance promise. Sales of the 524td, while close to plan, were relatively low, reflecting the public's waning fancy with oil burners. Interestingly, the eta-engined 528e, continues as a top seller for Munich in North America.

High-Performance 5-Series

The 5-Series has become the hotrod darling of the German tuners. First a 3.5, then the 545i (a turbo 3.5 liter) ensured that BMW's claim as the world's fastest sedan, period, remained unchallenged. Gray market importers are bringing in Alpina- and Hartge-tuned 5-Series

---

520/520i (1972-77). 520/6 (1977-81)

Engine
Type:. . . . . in-line. water-cooled 4. 6 (520/6)
Bore x Stroke (mm): 89x80. 80x66 (520/6)
Displacement (cc): 1990
Valve Operation:. . . . . sohc
Compression Ratio: . . . .9.0:1. 9.5:1 (i. 1972-75). 9.3:1 (i. 1975-77). 9.2:1 (520/6)
Carburetion: . . . . twin Stromberg 175CDET/Kugelfischer Mechanical fuel injection(i). Solex 4A1 (520/6)
BHP (mfr DIN): . . . . 115@5800. 120@5700(i). 122@6000 (520/6)
Chassis and Drivetrain
Transmission:4-speed manual or 3-speed automatic. 4-speed manual (i)
Steering: . . . . worm & roller
Front Suspension: . . . . MacPherson struts. coil springs. antiroll bar
Rear Suspension:. . . semitrailing arms. coil springs. antiroll bar (bar was optional on 520/6)
Axle Ratio:. 4.11. 3.90 (520i. 520/6)
General
Wheelbase (mm/in): 2636/103.0
Track front/rear (mm/in): 1406/1442-55.4/56.8
Brakes:. . . . . disc. drum
Wheels/Tires: . . . . . 14x5½J/175SR-14. 175HR-14(i). 175SR-14 (520/6)
Units Produced: . . total 5-Series through December 31. 1978. was 467.112
Maximum speed (kph/mph): . . . . . 175/109. 181/112(i. 520/6)
Notes: 520/520i's were not produced for North America. When the 6-cylinder 520 was introduced in 1977. the 4's were dropped. The 520-Series design set a precedent for future medium-sized BMW sedans.

525/528

Engine
Type:. . . . . in-line. water-cooled 6
Bore x Stroke (mm): 86x71.6. 86x80 (528)
Displacement (cc): 2494. 2788 (528)
Valve Operation: . . . . sohc
Compression Ratio: 9.0:1
Carburetion: . . . . .twin Zenith 32/40 INAT. twin Zenith 35/40 INAT (528): after August 1976. one Solex 4A1 (525 & 528)
BHP (mfr DIN): . . . . 145@6000. after August 1976. 150@5800 (525): 165@5800 (528). after August 1976. 170@5800
Chassis and Drivetrain
Transmission:. . . . . . . .4-speed manual or 3-speed automatic
Steering: . . . . worm & roller (power assist optional)
Front Suspension: . . . . MacPherson struts. coil springs. antiroll bar
Rear Suspension:. . . . . semitrailing arms. coil springs. antiroll bar
Axle Ratio:. 3.64
General
Wheelbase (mm/in): 2636/103.0
Track front/rear (mm/in): 1406/1442-55.4/56.8
Brakes:. . . . . disc/disc
Wheels/Tires: . . . . 14x5½J/175HR-14. 14x65/195/70HR-14 (528) 195/70 HR-14 optional
Units Produced: . . total 5-Series through December 31. 1978. was 467.112
Maximum speed (kph/mph): 192/119
Notes: The 525 and 528 are still in production in Europe. For North America. the 528i eventually replaced the 530i. In 1977 and in 1982. the 5-Series cars were extensively faceflifted. Currently an eta-engined 525e is offered in Europe.

variants, but with the stock 535i a pretty hot number, you have to be relatively wealthy and a dyed-in-the-wool performance addict to want a still *faster* BMW in the US driving environment. Of course, if a 155 mph sedan's your dream, look no further!

The 5-Series cars continue to be manufactured by Munich, for European markets with 1.8, 2.0, 2.5 and 2.8 liter powerplants, ensuring that BMW's middle range retained its wide appeal and pricing balance.

Best buys in the 5-Series? I think a used 528i, despite its early styling, combines the best of performance and living space. Michel Potheau feels, and I agree, that "...a 530i with a new cylinder head costs the same as a 2002—forty to forty-five percent less than a 528i— and these should not be ignored as a real sports sedan bargain."

The once-steady rise of BMW prices has leveled, permitting new buyers, especially those seeking used cars, to catch up. Many 5-Series cars were leased by professionals and their three-year terms are up now, making them available for purchase. With the 530i/528i only marginally slower than a 533, the price difference gives you a lot of car for the money.

M535i

For the 1985 model year overseas, BMW brought back the M535i to please a selected group of performance sedan purchasers. Equipped with the ubiquitous 3.5 engine, the M535i has a higher state of tune than its already quick cousins. With 10.0:1 compression, the M535i develops 218 bhp (160 DIN) and a whopping 225 ft/lbs of torque at 4000 rpm. Buyers can choose from a 5-speed or the optional electro-hydraulic 4-speed automatic. A twenty-five-percent limited-slip differential is also standard equipment, as are sport shock absorbers and an uprated suspension package.

Popular in North America, the 528i cured the 530's ills and offered better performance with a smaller engine. These cars are a good buy today and are reliable and very quick. (Author photos)

530i

Engine

Type:	in-line, water-cooled 6
Bore x Stroke (mm):	89x80
Displacement (cc):	2985
Valve Operation:	sohc
Compression Ratio:	9:1
Carburetion:	Bosch L-Jetronic fuel injection
BHP (mfr SAE):	176@5500

Chassis and Drivetrain

Transmission:	4-speed manual or 3-speed automatic
Steering:	power-assisted worm & roller
Front Suspension:	MacPherson struts, coil springs
Rear Suspension:	semitrailing arms, coil springs
Axle Ratio:	3.45

General

Wheelbase (mm/in):	2536/103.0
Track front/rear (mm/in):	1422/1460-56.0/57.5
Brakes:	disc/disc
Wheels/Tires:	14x6J/195/70HR-14
Units Produced:	27,870
Maximum speed (kph/mph):	194/120

Notes: This was the first BMW model created solely for the North American market. A bigger 3-liter engine was specified so EPA equipment would not stunt the 528i's performance. The 530i's thermal reactor emissions control system was a problem source. The 530i received the 5-Series line facelift in 1977, including reduced gas tank capacity (2 gallons less).

The M535i turns 0-60 in a shade over seven seconds and winds out to 143 mph—a nice improvement over the 'cooking' 535i. Inside, sport buckets and the M-Technics three-spoke steering wheel make aggressive driving comfortable. Standard equipment ABS brakes, of course, and TRX tires on special lightweight rims are also part of the specification. Knowledgeable autobahn racers look for the little M-Sport badges, rear spoiler, deep front air dam and side skirts to distinguish BMW's mid-range four-door Q-ship. As this is written, there are no plans to import the M535i into North America, but gray marketers have converted quite a few.

M5

BMW's quickest and most agile sedan is yet another variation on the 5-Series, the subtle but oh-so-quick M5. With only 250 of these largely hand-assembled sport sedans planned each year, the first allotment was quickly swept away by eager Europeans who wanted the comfort of four seats at over,150 mph.

Under the M5's hood lurks an old BMW friend, the 286 bhp four-valve twin-cam killer motor we loved in the M635CSi. Driven through a choice of close-ratio Getrag or ZF five-speeds, the big six makes a shambles of 0-60 times (6.3 seconds) and, according to *AutoWeek*, outruns a Lotus Esprit Turbo—with a quartet of friends enjoying the Blaupunkt stereo!

The chassis has been especially upgraded to handle the M5's capability, with bigger front brakes and a redesigned ABS system. The oversized Michelins on alloy wheels also help the M5 stick closely to the road at sub-sonic speeds.

In terms of looks, the M5 is even more subtle than the M535i, and many buyers opt to omit the BMW Motorsport badges, to disguise the car even more. At the Motorsport facility, located a short drive from the BMW factory in Munich, an engineer told me many of the M5 customers are well-to-do Germen businessman who wanted to be able to run away and hide from almost anything they'd encounter on the autobahn. "They don't have to advertise that they have a fast car," he said, "they just like knowing they have it."

Gray marketers have handled a few M5's, as there are no plans on the part of BMW NA to bring in their devil sedan. But, if the M635CSi sells as planned, perhaps the Montvale crowd will reconsider the fleet four-door for North America.

```
                    M-5
Engine
Type:.....................in-line, water-cooled 6
Bore x Stroke (mm):...................93.4x84
Displacement:.........................3453
Valve Operation:...........dohc, 24-valve head
Compression Ratio:....................10.5:1
Carburetion:.......Digital Motor Electronics fuel injection
BHP (mfr DIN/SAE):.............210/286@6400
Chassis and Drivetrain
Transmission:.....5-speed manual (choice of Getralt OD or
  ZF close-ratio sports)
Front Suspension:.........independent, with double joint
  control arm strut, coil springs, antiroll bar
Rear Suspension:.....independent, with semitrailing arms,
  coil springs, antiroll bar
Axle Ratio:........................3.73:1. (25% LSD)
General
Wheelbase (mm/in):.................2625/103.3
Track front/rear (mm/in):.........1430/1465-56.3/57.7
Brakes:..........................disc/disc (ABS)
Wheels/Tires:....165 TR 390 aluminum alloy 220/55 VR 390
Units Produced:.............(currently in production)
Maximum Speed (kph/mph):...............245/148
Notes: For Europe only, there are currently no plans to import
  the hyper-quick, deceptive-looking M-5.
```

```
                    M535i
Engine
Type:.....................in-line, water-cooled 6
Bore x Stroke (mm):.....................92x86
Displacement (cc):.......................3430
Valve Operation:..........................sohc
Compression Ratio:.......................10.0:1
Carburetion:...........Bosch Motronic fuel injection
BHP (mfr DIN/SAE):..............160/218@5500
Chassis and Drivetrain
Transmission:....5-speed manual (choice of 2 od or sports)
  or 4-speed automatic (electro-hydraulic control optional)
Steering:............power-assisted ball and nut
Front Suspension:........MacPherson struts, coil springs,
  antiroll bar
Rear Suspension:.........semitrailing arms, coil springs,
  antiroll bar
Axle Ratio:.......................3.07 (25% LSD)
General
Wheelbase (mm/in):.................2625/103.3
Track front/rear (mm/in):.........1430/1465-56.3/57.7
Brakes:..........................disc/disc (ABS)
Wheels/Tires:....165 TR 390 aluminum alloy 220/55 VR 390
Units Produced:.............(currently in production)
Maximum Speed (kph/mph):...............230/143
Notes: A Europe only model, the M-535i is a revival of an
  early seventies BMW road rocket.
```

1983-84 528e featured styling update, new type of alloy wheels; resemblance to earliest 5-Series cars was evident. (BMW NA photo)

On the road near the Rhine, this European 528i had standard bumpers, built-in fog lights, cleaner front end appearance. (Author photo)

528i/M535i

Engine
Type: .... in-line. water-cooled 6
Bore x Stroke (mm): 86x80. 93.4x84 (M535i)
Displacement (cc): 2788. 3453 (M535i)
Valve Operation: .... sohc
Compression Ratio: 9.3:1
Carburetion: .... Bosch L-Jetronic fuel injection
BHP (mfr DIN/SAE): ..... 176@5800 (US version 169@5500). 218@5200 (M535i)

Chassis and Drivetrain
Transmission: .. 4- or 5-speed manual or 3-speed automatic. 5-speed manual (M535i)
Steering: .... power-assisted worm & roller. power-assisted recirculating ball (M535i)
Front Suspension: .... MacPherson struts. coil springs
Rear Suspension: .... semitrailing arms. coil springs
Axle Ratio: .... 3.45 (528i). 3.25 or 3.07 (M535i)

General
Wheelbase (mm/in): 2536/103.0
Track front/rear (mm/in): 1422/1470-56.0/57.9
Brakes: .... disc
Wheels/Tires: 14x6J/195/70HR-14. 14x6½J/195/70VR-14 (M535i)
Units Produced: ..... Still in production in Europe. Total US 528i units 1977-81 were 19.710
Maximum speed (kph/mph): ...... 208/129. 202/125 or 219/130 (M535i)
Notes: The US 528i suffered slightly from its emission controls, but performance still beat the 530i. Dropped in 1981, for the 528e, the 5-Series fast reputation was renewed by the 533i in 1982. BMW is currently selling a new M535i in Europe. 528i European model, 1981-present; M535i European model, 1979-80.

For Europe only, exciting M-535i never made it officially to North America. Purposeful air dam, wide wheels, rocket motor with handling to match would have dismayed the DOT and EPA inspectors. (BMW Werkfoto)

Fast-paced 533i brought BMW performance back to the US and blew off every other sedan in the process. The 181 bhp six took no prisoners. TRX tires on specially-sized wheels were distinctive. Note directionals in bumpers; fog lamps underneath. (BMW NA photo)

New in '83 in Europe, 2 years later in North America, the diesel-powered 524td was virtually indistinguishable externally from the rest of the 5-Series. Steel wheels and trim details here are a giveaway. (BMW NA photo)

528e/533i/524td/535i

Engine

Type:..... in-line, water-cooled 6 (528e, 533i), turbocharged diesel (524td)

Bore x Stroke (mm): ... 84.1x81.0 (528e), 89x86 (533i), 80x81 (524td)

Displacement (cc): 2693 (528e), 3210 (533i), 2443 (524td), 3430 (535i)

Valve Operation:....... sohc (528e), sohc (533i), n/a (524td)

Compression Ratio: 9.0:1 (528e), 8.8:1 (533i), 22.0:1 (524td), 8.0:1 (535i)

Carburetion: ..... Bosch L-Jetronic (528e), Bosch L-Jetronic (533i), n/a (524td)

BHP (mfr SAE): .... 121@4250 (528e), 181@6000 (533i), 115@4800 (524td), 182@5400 (535i)

Chassis and Drivetrain

Transmission:........5-speed manual or 3-speed automatic (528e, 533i), 5-speed manual or 4-speed automatic (524td)

Steering: .... power-assisted rack & pinion

Front Suspension: .... MacPherson struts, coil springs, antiroll bar

Rear Suspension: ...semitrailing arms, coil springs, (antiroll bar, only 533i)

Axle Ratio:.............2.93 (528e), 3.25 (533i), 3.15 (524td), 5.25 (535i)

General

Wheelbase (mm/in): 2625/103.3

Track front/rear (mm/in): 1430/1470-56.3/57.9

Brakes: .... disc/disc

Wheels/Tires: 6x14/195/70-14 (528e), 165TR390/200/60x390 (533i), 5½J-14/175HR-14 (524td)

Units Produced: ....Still in production. US 528e units 1981-82: 19,248; US 533i Units 1982-on: 4,108

Maximum speed (kph/mph): 184/114 (528e), 215/134 (533i), 179/111 (524td), 131 (535i)

Notes: 528e introduced in North America in 1982; the 533i was introduced in 1983; and the 524td, after a 1983 European introduction, entered the US market in late 1984. 535i (US) produced 1985 to present. 535i has Bosch Motronic fuel injection, ABS brakes standard.

The BMW 535i is equipped with the powerful 3.5 liter engine, giving the mid-sized sport sedan a 0-60 mph acceleration time of 7.4 seconds. Anti-lock braking system (ABS) gives a dramatic improvement in braking safety.

North American 528i in action. This 1980 version had a five-speed
manual as standard equipment. (BMW NA photo)

1982 528e sedan was scarcely greeted enthusiastically in North
America. Buffs thought the performance had disappeared. In fact
the e-model was plenty fast to 100 mph, performed best in the
below-70 range and was a better seller than any 5-Series before
it. (BMW NA photo)

Alas, only in Europe or through the gray marketers, BMW's delectable M535i has the looks and the scoring punch to make mincemeat of the fast lane. Deep, slotted front air dam, side skirts and a deck spoiler are visual clues. If you see the M-Sport badge in your mirror, be prepared for a challenge.

Look again, this subtle box is BMW's top contribution to the high-speed saloon market. The M5 grille and deck lid insignia quietly identify Munich's fastest four-door. The M-Sport, specially built, dohc 286 bhp six was termed by *AutoWeek*, ". . . the ultimate BMW sleeper car."

For 1985, the 535i. Ten percent more torque and standard ABS braking ensured this fleet sedan had the measure of everything in its class in North America. Oversized wheels, the deck i.d. and twin pipes are the surface clues for car spotters.

628CSi 1979- ★★✦
630CS 1976-79 ★★★
633CSi (US 1976-1984) ★★★
635CSi (E 1979-) ★★★★
M635CSi (E 1983-) ★★★★✦
635CSi (US 1985-) ★★★★

By 1976, when the oil crisis subsided, BMW was waiting with an exciting new coupe design: the new 6-Series. On a 1-mm-longer wheelbase, it was longer, lower and wider than its predecessors, setting another new standard for personal luxury cars that remains a yardstick today.

Closely following the 7-Series sedan improvements, the coupe's wider track, updated brakes and optional ZF automatic transmission were just a few of the new features. Power steering was standard with a variable-ratio, a feature that ensured high-speed "feel" and lessened hydraulic support as engine speed increased.

In restriction-free Europe, the new 630CS was equipped with a three-liter 185 bhp engine. Carburetion was handled by a big, four-barrel Solex. High rollers, of course, could opt for its successor, the 630 in injected form, followed by the 628CSi in 1979 or go for a bigger-bore version, the 633 CSi with its 200 bhp 3210 cc powerplant. By the time the new CSi made it to America, the car had lost nearly 24 bhp. The three-liter CSi was sold in the US for just one year (1977), and the 3.3 liter engine was the coupe's powerplant from 1978 onward.

The results were predictable: The Eurocoupe took only eight seconds to 60 mph, another seventeen to 100 and it topped out at 135. The US version was out of breath at 125. Ironically, the strength of the Mark made the cost of the slower US version (at about $25,000) much more expensive than its quicker German cousin.

In 1978, recognizing the performance disparity, Munich's engineers boosted the 6-Series compression ratio and redesigned the combustion chambers for a big lift in torque at lower rpm. As a result, the American car regained some of the maker's original punch.

Originally available only overseas, the 635CSi had a detuned version of the racing engine (two valves/cylinder and sohc versus a four-valve dohc configuration) with a 218 bhp rating. Sporting drivers on the Continent could opt for a five-speed gearbox, too. This combination topped 140 and blew the doors off anything in its class. The factory is also offering a Europe-only M635CSi M88 with four-valve 286 bhp killer motor. This car is probably the ultimate 6-Series example and it comes with fat, fifteen-inch alloys, 220/55 TRX's, big big floating caliper ventilated discs and a new, specially-geared five-speed backed by a limited-slip differential. This car will hit sixty in 6.4 seconds and will wail all the way to 160! Recently Georg Kacher of *Autoweek* spent some time in an M-type. While he could drift along at 1300 rpm in fifth (the "double nickel"), I suspect he spent most of his time on the autobahn chasing Ferraris. Standard equipment (for about $34,000 in Germany) is an ABS braking system, along with special wheels, bucket seats and all of BMW's usual electronic gadgetry.

As a postscript, it should be noted that the coupe, like most BMW's, has seen a subtle target-market change over the years. It has lost some of its sporting edge, particularly in the US where it has become an expensive two- and four-passenger status symbol. Coach Builders Ltd., Inc., of High Springs, Florida, even markets a full convertible version of the 6-Series

European BMW's came in many coupe variations: 628CSi, 633CSi and 635CSi with 184 bhp, 197 bhp and 218 bhp, respectively. European cars didn't require the extended bumpers and side lights, saving weight and helping aerodynamics. (BMW Werkfoto)

for $8,900 over the original sticker. Before you rush for your checkbook, bear in mind that this price is *dealer list* for the conversion and most buyers can expect to pay a great deal more.

Late in 1984, BMW launched the 635i in the US. Finally, luxury coupe purchasers didn't have to take a performance back seat. The 182 bhp, 3430 cc powerplant has ten percent more torque and 3.45:1 rear end ratio to use the newly found power. Computer-controlled anti-lock (ABS) brakes are standard and a front air dam (like the Euro-models) remind others that the new 6-Series is a performer once again.

The 6-Series appeals today to a mature, wealthy individual who knows he or she doesn't have to challenge anyone, and it can quickly turn from boulevardier to purposeful sports coupe. The car speaks eloquently for itself. In Germany, the factory racing division and tuning firms like Alpina offer hotter versions (Alpina has a twin-turbo) to transform the coupe into a holy terror in the CSL tradition.

630CS (1976-79)

Engine
Type:........................... in-line. water-cooled 6
Bore x Stroke (mm):........................... 89x80
Displacement (cc):...........................2985
Valve Operation:................................... sohc
Compression Ratio:........................... 9.0:1
Carburetion:........................... one Solex 4AI
BHP (mfr DIN):...........................185@5800

Chassis and Drivetrain
Transmission:........4-speed manual or 3-speed automatic
Steering:.............. recirculating ball. power-assisted
Front Suspension:........ MacPherson struts. coil springs. antiroll bar
Rear Suspension:.......... semitrailing arms. coil springs
Axle Ratio:................... (s) 3.45 (25% LSD optional)

General
Wheelbase (mm/in):........................... 2626/103.4
Track front/rear (mm/in):............1422/1487-56.0/58.5
Brakes:................................... disc/disc
Wheels/Tires:...................... 14x6J/195/70VR-14
Maximum speed (kph/mph):.........................210/130
Notes: Combined sales for calendar years 1978-82 for 6-Series were 32.292. US sales for 630/633 CSI from 1977-83 were 8.785.

630CSi

Engine
Type:........................... in-line. water-cooled 6
Bore x Stroke (mm):........................... 89x80
Displacement (cc):...........................2985
Valve Operation:................................... sohc
Compression Ratio:........................... 9.0:1
Carburetion:........................... Bosch L-Jetronic
BHP (mfr SAE):...........................176@5500

Chassis and Drivetrain
Transmission:........4-speed manual or 3-speed automatic
Steering:.............. recirculating ball. power-assisted
Front Suspension:........ MacPherson struts. coil springs. antiroll bar
Rear Suspension:... semitrailing arms. coil springs. antiroll bar
Axle Ratio (s):................... 3.45 (25% LSD optional)

General
Wheelbase (mm/in):........................... 2626/103.4
Track front/rear (mm/in):............1422/1487-56.0/58.5
Brakes:................................... disc/disc
Wheels/Tires:......................14x6½J/195/70HR-14
Units Produced:........ Combined sales for calendar years 1978-82 for 6-Series were 32.292. US sales for 630/633 CSi from 1977-83 were 8.785.
Maximum speed (kph/mph):.........................197/122
Notes: European 628CSi featured 9.3:1 compression. 80x86 mm. 2788 cc engine developing 184 bhp @ 5800. Top speed. 132 mph.

The 630CS and CSi were launched in early 1976 in Europe with the 633CSi becoming the North American version. From the side, European models were identical, with trunk badges proclaiming the injected models. (BMW Werkfoto)

This 630CSi shows off its 5 mph bumpers, integrated front side lights and added-on rear running lights. The federalized US version put out 177 bhp versus the European car's healthy 200 bhp. (BMW NA photo)

The US 633CSi shows the coupe's clean lines, the optional sunroof and one interesting owner-added accessory: a Callaway turbocharger conversion. (Author photos)

Side view of late 633CSi shows rear-marker lights incorporated into the extended bumper. BBS wheels were a later factory addition. (Author photo)

628CSi was popular in Europe—still packs a punch despite reduced displacement. (BMW Werkfoto)

633CSi

Engine

Type:........................... in-line, water-cooled 6
Bore x Stroke (mm): 89x86
Displacement (cc):.................................3210
Valve Operation:...................................... sohc
Compression Ratio: .. in US: 1978 9:1, 1979-81 8:1, 1982 8.8:1
Carburetion: .... Bosch L-Jetronic
BHP (mfr DIN/SAE): . 200@5500/177@5500 (1978), 176@5200
 (1979-81), 181@6000 (1982)

Chassis and Drivetrain

Transmission:....... 4-speed manual or 3-speed automatic.
 5-speed manual (1982-present)
Steering: .... recirculating ball, power-assisted
Front Suspension: .... MacPherson struts, coil springs,
 antiroll bar

Rear Suspension:......semitrailing arms, coil springs, anti-roll bar
Axle Ratio (s):....3.45 (25% LSD optional, 3.07 optional with
 25% LSD)

General

Wheelbase (mm/in): 2626/103.4
Track front/rear (mm/in): 1422/1487-56.0/58.5
Brakes:.. disc/disc
Wheels/Tires: 14x6½J/195/70VR-14
Units Produced: ....Still in production (see 630CSi)
Maximum speed (kph/mph): .... 215/133 (US 200/124)
Notes: EPA-regulated US cars have less horsepower than
 European counterparts.

North American 633CSi was an elegant tourer. Twin mirrors, luxo interior, new alloy wheel design helped make up for the coupe's lack of scat. (BMW NA photo)

European muscle: 635CSi, a 140 mph GT that earned a lot of autobahn respect. This quick coupe, in only slightly slower (132 mph) form, is a contender on US highways. Rear spoiler is not available on North American cars. (BMW Werkfoto)

This coupe can go. . . . Nelson Piquet relaxes beside the killer M635-CSi. BMW Motorsport's not-so-subtle modifications to this twin-cam terror make it a very desirable bolide. (BMW Werkfoto)

Flat out in a curve, the 286 bhp M635 has a top speed of just under 160. (BMW Werkfoto)

The fat, three-spoked wheel and 8000 rpm redline underscored the M635CSi's purpose. Twin cam, four-valve injected six was a direct descendant of the M1. (BMW Werkfoto)

Beefing up the US Sixer, the 1985 model year saw the intro of the 3.5 liter engine and ABS brakes. Buyers can choose between a Getrag five-speed or four-speed automatic. The list of standard equipment is a single-spaced page. BMW's new electronically controlled four-speed automatic and a limited-slip differential are the only options. (BMW NA)

A convertible 633CSi—clever cutting by Florida's Coach Builders, Ltd., Inc., converted the coupe into an open-air delight. (Courtesy Larry Moran)

6-Series early dash set precedent for later cars: It carried enclosed cockpit theme for these while introducing check control system. (BMW Werkfoto)

635CSi/M635CSi

Engine

Type: . . . . in-line, water-cooled 6
Bore x Stroke (mm): . . . . 93.4x84.0, 92.0x86.0 (US)
Displacement (cc): . . . . 3453, 3430 (US)
Valve Operation: . . . . sohc, dohc (M635CSi)
Compression Ratio: . . . . 9.3:1, 9.0:1 (M635CS), 8.0:1 (US)
Carburetion: . . . . Bosch L-Jetronic fuel injection
BHP (mfr DIN): . . . . 218@5200, 286@6500 (M635CSi), 182@5400 (US)

Chassis and Drivetrain

Transmission: . . . . 5-speed manual
Steering: . . . . power-assisted recirculating ball
Front Suspension: . . . . MacPherson struts, coil springs, antiroll bar
Rear Suspension: . . . . semitrailing arms, coil springs, antiroll bar
Axle Ratio: . . . . 3.25 (25% LSD), 3.07 (optional 25% LSD M635CSi), 3.45 w/LSD opt. (US)

General

Wheelbase (mm/in): 2526/103.4
Track front/rear (mm/in): 1422/1487-56.0/58.5
Brakes: . . . . disc/disc (antiskid braking is optional)
Wheels/Tires: . . . . 14x6½J/195/70VR-14, TRX220/55VR390 (M635CSi), 220/55 390 (US)
Units Produced: . . . Still in production; began 1978, M635CSi began 1983
Maximum speed (kph/mph): . . . 225/140, 254/158 (M635CSi), 220/132 (US)
Notes: The 635CSi in standard or M form has not been imported by BMW to North America. The CSi's lowered suspension, spoilers (front only in US) and wide wheels clearly mark it as a sports tourer. Bosch Motronic fuel injection and standard ABS brakes on US.

728/i 1977-79 ★★
730 1977-79 ★★
733i 1977- ★★★⌐
732i (E 1979-) ★★★★
735i (E 1979-) ★★★★
735 (US 1985-) ★★★★
745i (E 1979-) ★★★★⌐

E stands for Europe-only models

BMW introduced its largest line of sedans in January 1977. Succeeding the 2500/2800/3.0/ 3.3 models, the big, new four-door sported an intentional family resemblance. It topped its previously biggest predecessor by a 3-mm-longer wheelbase as well as contemporary sheet metal whose breadth exceeded the older models in every dimension.

The 7-Series cars, while not really collector items, typified BMW's serious approach to the luxury market and offered a realistic (and much faster for the money) alternative to Mercedes. Elegant touches like fully integrated air conditioning, wide orthopedic-inspired seats, even a built-in first aid kit were standard. European cars even had electrically operated *rear* seats.

The chassis and running gear had their share of special attributes, too, like doubly pivoted antidive front suspension and powerful hydraulically assisted four-wheel disc brakes. Selected powertrain refinements ensured the 7-Series continues to earn its top spot in the Munich range.

Initially, the 728 (170 bhp) and 730 (184 bhp) carbureted versions carried the flag, later augmented by a 3.3 liter injected variation, the 733i. In July 1979, fuel injection became standard on all the engine sizes. In Germany and other European countries, the 733i logically gave way in 1979 to the 732i. An enlarged addition, the 735i, was also available only in Europe. The ultimate factory performance king was the 745i—again just for overseas unless you were able to afford gray market importing.

The 745i first appeared in 1980 and has been revised every year since. The designation sprang from a formula which used a factor of 1.4 multiplied by the engine capacity to establish the international racing classification for turbocharged cars.

The big 7's 3210 cc injected six was turbocharged by a KKK unit which, combined with fuel injection, helped push the engine's power rating to 252 bhp (DIN) at 5200. Coupled with a 280-pounds-feet torque rating (at 2600 rpm), this 3,500-pound sedan ran from 0-60 in under eight seconds, and topped out over 140 mph. In the latest variation, although horse-power was unchanged, displacement was up to 3.5 liters but the power was developed at 4900 rpm and the torque figure, 275 pounds-feet, came on at a lower 2200 revs.

Of course, a modified sport suspension was added and the three revisions were pro-gressively designed to ensure that tail-happiness was reduced in this big charger.

Thos. L. Bryant, of *Road & Track*, drove a second-series 745i and commented: "The sport suspension changes the 7-Series sedan from a very good handling car to a superb one. The moderate body roll found in the 733i, for example, disappears almost completely and the 745i exhibits a steadiness that is inspiring."

Writing for *Autoweek*, Georg Kacher drove a new third-series 745i with these impres-sions: "The Mark III accelerates from 0-60 in 7.9 seconds and can reach a top speed of 143 mph." Kacher wasn't impressed with the new suspension modifications, however. "Earlier 7-Series models either offered acceptable ride comfort or acceptable roadholding qualities,

From its introduction, the BMW 7-Series set new luxury-car standards in its class. Styling was similar to the newer 6-Series coupes.
German buyers opted for carbureted 2.8 and three-liter variations,
as well as the injected 733i (really a 3.2 liter). Europeans also got
seven-inch low-beam lighting (in the US, headlamps have to be
the same size). This European car had smaller bumpers (US version is fitted with 5-mph-impact bumpers) and V-rated Michelin
XWX tires. (BMW Werkfoto)

but the new 745i doesn't excel in either respect. Driven fast, the big Bimmer hangs its tail out disappointingly early calling for a quick and generous dose of opposite lock."

In South Africa, the 745i is available with the twenty-four-valve M injected engine instead of the turbo. South Africans can order this car as the 735i.

In America, the 733i was the only version of the big car officially available until late 1984. Now, as the 735i, it is marketed with all the latest modifications like newly designed alloys, TRX tires, an on-board computer and the ABS braking system. German buyers have a 197 bhp 732i while Americans still have to be content with nearly fifteen fewer horsepower. A new American 735i variant for 1986, the L7, includes a luxurious leather interior and driver's side airbag as standard equipment.

The 7 certainly reached BMW's initial expectations: Over 30,000 cars were sold in the first three years of production. As big high-speed sedans, these cars, with their continual refinements, represented very good value. Always in pursuit of Mercedes-Benz, BMW's competitive spirit frequently inspired the company to improve on the specifications.

As a postscript to the 7-Series, Alpina in Germany and Garage du Bac in France offer cleverly-built station wagons on the 7 platform. The Alpina company will fit one of its shooting brakes with a full B9 high-performance engine and suspension for the ultimate in fast freight! While the value of this type of custom conversion might not increase over time, it's hard to beat this combination for prestige and rarity.

Where will the 7-Series go? Some years ago the factory experimented with a twelve-cylinder engine, a 4.5 liter motor that was abandoned in 1978 when the fuel crisis seemed to be of epidemic proportions. The 7-Series is due for a facelift for the 1987 model year. As we went to press, it seemed evident that a newly designed 4.7 liter V-12 was being tested—as a competitive way to upgrade BMW's big sixes making them equal to Mercedes eights. The twelve could be the ultimate trump card in 1987. That's not too surprising, perhaps, from a company that still values its reputation among enthusiasts!

728/728i

Engine
Type: . . . . in-line water-cooled 6
Bore x Stroke (mm): 86x80
Displacement (cc): 2788
Valve Operation: . . . . sohc
Compression Ratio: 9.0:1
Carburetion: . . . . Solex 4 Al/Bosch L-Jetronic
BHP (mfr DIN): . . . . .170@5800
Chassis and Drivetrain
Transmission: . . . . .4-speed manual or 3-speed automatic
  (after 1982. 5-speed manual)
Steering: . . . . power-assisted recirculating ball
Front Suspension: . . . . MacPherson struts. coil springs.
  antiroll bar
Rear Suspension: . . . . semitrailing arms. coil springs
Axle Ratio: 3.64
General
Wheelbase (mm/in): 2795/110.0
Track front/rear (mm/in): 1508/1522-59.4/59.9
Brakes: . . . . disc/disc
Wheels/Tires: 6Jx14/195/70HR-14
Units Produced: . . . . Factory data does not distinguish
  between model and calendar year production for current
  series.* 728 produced from 1977-79; 728i still in production.
Maximum speed (kph/mph): 192/119
*Total 7-Series cars produced between 1978-82 were 164.299.
  US 7-Series units. from 1979-83. total was 16.184.

730/732/732i

Engine
Type: . . . . in-line. water-cooled 6
Bore x Stroke (mm): . . . . 89x80 (730). 89x86 (732. 732i)
Displacement (cc): . . . . .2985 (730). 3210 (732. 732i)
Valve Operation: . . . . sohc
Compression Ratio: 9.0:1. 9.3:1 (732i)
Carburetion: . . . . Solex 4 Al/Bosch L-Jetronic
BHP (mfr DIN): . . . . 184@5800/197@5500 (732i)
Chassis and Drivetrain
Transmission: . . . . .4-speed manual or 3-speed automatic
  (after 1982. 5-speed manual)
Steering: . . . . power-assisted recirculating ball
Front Suspension: . . . . MacPherson struts. coil springs.
  antiroll bar
Rear Suspension: . . . . semitrailing arms. coil springs
Axle Ratio: 3.45
General
Wheelbase (mm/in): 2795/110.0
Track front/rear (mm/in): 1508/1522-59.4/59.9
Brakes: . . . . disc/disc
Wheels/Tires: 6½Jx14/205/70HR-14
Units Produced: . . . . Factory data does not distinguish
  between model and calendar year production for current
  series.*
Maximum speed (kph/mph): 200/124
Notes: These models were not imported into North America.
  * Total 7-Series cars produced between 1978-82 were 164.299.
  US 7-Series units. from 1979-1983. total was 16.184.

7-Series dash befit a luxury cruiser—built-ins included just about everything. (BMW Werkfoto)

From the side, the 7-Series was graceful for a large car. Driven with verve, the big sedan had all the characteristics of its more sporting brethren. Alloy wheels covered four-wheel disc brakes. (BMW Werkfoto)

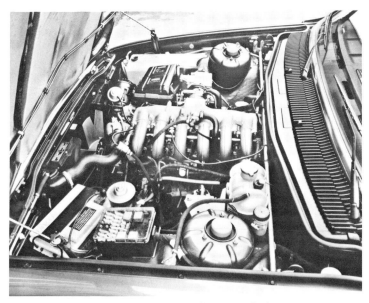

The 733i powerplant—a smooth six many feel was the best of its configuration in the world. Bosch L-Jetronic fuel injection replaced Solex carburetion on earlier cars. Later 735i's have Bosch Motronic fuel injection. (BMW Werkfoto)

Photographed in the Netherlands, this 745i showed off its new wheels with TRX low-profile tires. (BMW Werkfoto)

733i/735i

Engine

Type: . . . . in-line, water-cooled 6
Bore x Stroke (mm): 89x86, 92x86 (735i)
Displacement (cc): 3210, 3430 (735i)
Valve Operation: . . . . sohc
Compression Ratio: . . . . .9.0:1 (US 1982 8.8:1), 8.0:1 (735i)
Carburetion: . . . . Bosch L-Jetronic
BHP (mfr DIN/SAE): . . 1979-81 197@5500, 1982-83 181@6200,
  182@5400 (735i)

Chassis and Drivetrain

Transmission: . . . . .4-speed manual or 3-speed automatic
  (before 1982), 5-speed manual or 3-speed automatic
Steering: . . . . power-assisted recirculating ball
Front Suspension: . . . . MacPherson struts, coil springs,
  antiroll bar
Rear Suspension: . . . . .semitrailing arms, coil springs
Axle Ration: . . . . . US 3.45, 1982 3.25, 3.45 w/opt. LSD (735i)

General

Wheelbase (mm/in): 2795/110.0
Track front/rear (mm/in): 1508/1522-59.4/59.9
Brakes: . . . . disc/disc
Wheels/Tires: 6½Jx14/205/70VR-14, 205/70VR14
  (735i)
Units Produced: . . . . Factory data does not distinguish
  between model and calendar year production for current
  series.*
Notes: European 733i's were produced from 1977-79, replaced
  in 1978 by the 735i. Data for North American 735i, which
  has Bosch Motronic fuel injection, standard ABS
  brakes and maximum speed of 209kph/125mph.
* Total 7-Series cars produced between 1978-82 were 164,299.
  US 7-Series units, from 1979-1983, total was 16,184.

A 735i parked on a quiet street near Juan-Les-Pins, France. For the buyer wanting a little more power, the 3.5 liter variation on the six-cylinder theme (available only in Europe) was the answer. (Author photo)

North American 7-Series had big impact bumpers, equalized lighting, new alloy wheel design. (BMW NA photo)

For 1986, BMW updated its long-in-the-tooth big sedan with ABS braking, the carried-over 3.5 liter six and an optional electronically controlled automatic transmission. Unlike its rivals, the big 500-Series Mercs, the BMW is the only really big sedan still available with a five-speed—and it's a great treat to drive when you can stir the speeds yourself. (BMW NA)

Latest North American-bound 7-Series cars have redesigned noses and grilles, and a series of subtle aerodynamic styling refinements. The North American 735i is equipped with fog lamps under the bumpers. (BMW NA photo)

745i's in North America—gray marketers (or compliance importers as they prefer to be called) will make them available. Prices are competitive with BMW-imported 735i's. Risks include lack of spares if you're far from an importer. Specialists like Hardy & Beck and Teves Performance make it a simple, rewarding procedure to own one of these autobahn bullets. (Courtesy Phil Teves, Teves Performance)

735i/745i

Engine
Type:....... in-line. water-cooled 6. (turbocharged for 745i)
Bore x Stroke (mm): 93.4x84. 89x86 (745i)
Displacement (cc): 3453. 3210 (745i)
Valve Operation:.................................... sohc
Compression Ratio: 9.3:1. 7.0:1 (745i)
Carburetion: .... Bosch L-Jetronic. Bosch L-Jetronic and KKK K27 turbocharger (745i)
BHP (mfr DIN): .... 218@5200. 252@5200 (745i)

Chassis and Drivetrain
Transmission:....... 5-speed manual or 3-speed automatic. 3-speed automatic (745i only)
Steering: .... power-assisted recirculating ball
Front Suspension: .... MacPherson struts. coil springs. antiroll bar

Rear Suspension:..... semitrailing arms. coil springs. Also. 745i has hydropneumatic self-leveling and antiroll bar
Axle Ratio:.............. 3.25/25%LSD. 3.07/25%LSD (745i)

General
Wheelbase (mm/in): 2795/110.0
Track front/rear (mm/in): 1502/1516-59.4/59.9
Brakes:.............. disc/disc. ABS antilock brakes (745i)
Wheels/Tires: .... 6½Jx14 205/70VR-14 or TRX 165TR390 and 220 55VR 390 tires
Units Produced: ....still in production
Maximum speed (kph/mph): 213/132. 224/138 (745i)
Notes: These cars are "officially" available only in Europe but some have been imported into the US. 745i is only available in Europe.

The most exotic road-going BMW? Unquestionably, the sleek M1. It's the car many enthusiasts thought would re-establish BMW's sports car reputation.

The M1 development actually began in 1972, when BMW unveiled its Turbo show car. The highly advanced Turbo had gullwing doors and a state-of-the-art, turbocharged two-liter-four East/West engine positioned amidships. Some of the styling touches, like a sculpted hood bulge tapering into a modernized twin-kidney grille opening, were adopted soon afterward for production Bimmers.

The initial response was enthusiastic, but no plans existed at the time to bring the Turbo (or a tamer production version) to market. BMW was working on the concept of a sports model, while cheerfully selling all the conventional cars it could manufacture.

The original Turbo was radical. The next evolution of the concept began to point the way toward a more practical successor. Ital Design and the brilliant Georgio Giugiaro were called in. Using the Turbo as a starting guideline, Giugiaro refined the silhouette even further. He proposed a fiberglass-bodied sportster with conventional doors. The powerplant was a dohc 3.5 liter six lifted from the CSL racing coupes.

The whole idea was beginning to gel. The car was originally called the E-26. But to correspond with the factory's then-current racing designations, it was renamed M1.

BMW management has always believed in the "racing improves the breed" adage. The company put a lot of money behind the notion that a successful racing effort would soundly underscore the performance of its street machines. The M1, with a choice of suitable engines, would be ideal for the Group 4 and 5 classes in European racing. The decision to competitively run the sleek coupes presented Munich with a challenge—and an opportunity.

FIA regulations demanded that 400 copies of the M1 be produced within a two-year period. The project was beyond the BMW factory's capability for this type of specialized car, so a complex but achievable manufacturing program was developed utilizing BMW's competition affiliate, Motorsports Gmbh in Munich. The racing subsidiary had worked on the prototype in conjunction with Ital Design; the first car had been built by an old hand at exotica: Lamborghini.

Lamborghini received the initial contract for the 400 M1's, but the Italian producer was unable to help. A shortage of cash and an abundance of labor problems intervened, making it necessary for Sant'Agata Bolognese to withdraw.

BMW was eager to continue but the resultant production scheme must have caused periodic fits among the systematic Germans. Here's how they did it:

An Italian firm called Marchesi welded together the M1 tubular space frame chassis. Exquisitely hand-formed fiberglass panels came from another Italian supplier, Transformazione Italiana Resina. The steel and plastic met at Ital Design where the subassemblies were built and painted. Then, the partially complete M1's were shipped to Baur, a Stuttgart coachbuilder that helped BMW with cabriolet versions of a number of models.

The craftsmen at Baur trimmed the bodies, added leather Recaros and installed the dohc six-cylinder engines, suspension and running gear. The cars were then shipped to Motorsport for final testing and a comprehensive quality check.

The ultimate road-going BMW, the M1. This supercar's sharp silhouette and distinctive form made it instantly recognizable. Imported only occasionally into the US, used M1's command astro-
nomical prices. (BMW Werkfoto)

Essentially a detuned racer, each M1 was thus a limited-production, virtually hand-built, rarity—packed with state-of-the-art technology. But the M1 had dash to go with the high-tech flash. The twenty-four-valve, fuel-injected 277 bhp engine produced six-second 0-60 times and the sophisticated double A-arm suspension, plus slick alloys with fat P-7's ensured there was handling to match.

Road & Track's Joe Rusz, a very capable driver, had an exciting experience in Germany following the 1980 Belgian Grand Prix when he drove an M1 from Zolder to Munich. "... it is a sunny May morning in Belgium and you have just booted the throttle to send the tach spinning wildly toward its 7000-rpm redline. Ah, the joy of electronic ignition. Here I was, minutes ago, lugging the engine in traffic. Yet, the sound is now loud and clear as third and fourth come and go. Now I'm in top and in the fast lane, cruising at 120 mph. The M1 has not even begun to extend itself, yet we are practically alone. Intimidated by the BMW or hindered by the stiff European gasoline prices, the Mercedes-Benz 450's and 500's, the BMW 733's and the occasional Porsche 911's and 928's keep their distance.

"Finally, as I pass through Aachen, a Golf GTi tucks in behind me. Although the VW is good for only 110 mph, he glues himself to my bumper in traffic, only to fall back when the road is clear. We have a nice romp until we get to a new stretch of Autobahn where there is sufficient room to unleash some of the BMW's power. When you're traveling that fast, even the clearest road seems cluttered with traffic. So I am frustrated by my environment that allows me to go only 145 mph instead of the 160-plus that represents the M1's actual top speed."

In 1982, when M1 production ended, a European car cost about $65,000. To land a federalized version in the states upped the ante to $110,000-115,000. BMW stopped production after 400 "street" M1's and twenty-six racers had been completed. Officially, the cars weren't intended for sale in the US, but a few cars were converted and they're relatively rare.

If an M1 is your dream, federalized conversions occasionally appear in *Road & Track* and *Autoweek* classifieds. Be sure the car is properly certified before you plunk down a high-five-figure check. Spares are available, mostly from Germany, as there are no US firms that specialize solely in M1's. Still, if you want the ultimate BMW and you have the means, this car is very tempting. As this is written, BMW has no plans for a successor to the M1, but I wouldn't bet on that lasting forever. . . .

M1

Engine

Type: . . . . in-line. water-cooled 6
Bore x Stroke (mm): 93.4/84.0
Displacement (cc): 3453
Valve Operation: . . . . dohc. 4 valves per cylinder
Compression Ratio: 9.0:1
Carburetion: . . Kugelfischer-Bosch mechanical fuel injection
BHP (mfr DIN): . . . . 277@6500

Chassis and Drivetrain

Transmission: . . . . 5-speed manual (transaxle)
Steering: . . . . rack & pinion
Front Suspension: . . . . . unequal-length A-arms. coil springs. antiroll bar
Rear Suspension: . . . . . . unequal-length A-arms. coil springs. antiroll bar

Axle Ratio: . . . . 4.22 (40% LSD)

General

Wheelbase (mm/in): 2560/100.8
Track front/rear (mm/in): 1550/1576-61.0/62.0
Brakes: . . . . disc/disc
Wheels/Tires: . . . . F: 16x7/205/55VR16. R: 16x8/225/50VR16
Units Produced: 450 (1978-80)
Maximum speed (kph/mph): 262/162
Notes: "Street" versions of the fiberglass-bodied M1 were never officially homologated for the US. but cars have been imported and converted. Racing M1's develop 470 bhp for Group 4 and the turbocharged Group 5 car has a 3.2 liter six developing approximately 850 bhp.

Viewed from ahead, the menacing M1 is low, mean and very, very fast. The M1's aggressive stance is still contemporary, still desirable. There aren't many cars that can stay ahead of this one. (BMW Werkfoto courtesy Halwart Schrader)

What constitutes a 163 mph car? Start with a four-valve twin-cam six amidships, add fuel injection, mix with disc ventilated brakes and a transaxle and head for an autobahn. The race-derived six is good for 277 bhp. (BMW Werkfoto)

Seen alongside the M635CSi, the fiberglass M1 traditional BMW
styling hallmarks are evident—in a futuristically inspired design.
Sadly, both cars are available in the US only through gray market
importers. (BMW Werkfoto)

The M1 cockpit was restrained, understated, plain but functional. Although it's been criticized as a rather dull command post for a luxury sports car, M1 devotees point out the 9000 rpm tach and 280 kph speedo as proof positive you can have quite a ride in this berlinetta. (BMW Werkfoto)

Fifty years of progress contrasted Group 4 M1 racer with the diminutive Dixi. Street M1's had fat P-7's on wide alloys, racing versions had even wider alloys, still fatter tires. (BMW Werkfoto)

RARE BMW'S

When BMW's postwar production began, limited funds and the high cost of special tooling kept model proliferation to a minimum. However, that didn't stop certain coachbuilders from experimenting, and staid carriage works like Baur in Stuttgart and Autenrieth in Darmstadt built catalog convertibles and coupes in small numbers. These are among the rarest early BMW's.

Others tried their hands, too, like Gebruder Beutler in Thun, Switzerland. The Beutler brothers built a postwar convertible on a prewar 328 chassis and contrived a bulbous coupe on the 502 V-8 platform. Later in 1962-63, they tried again with a four-seater coupe design on the 502 chassis that looked a bit like the Goertz 503.

Bertone, of course, had a hand in the 3200 design and even Pininfarina built a few special BMW's. Frua of Torino designed the Glas coupes and Michelotti was responsible for the 700-Series cars. Carozzeria Vignale, also in Turin, built one special-bodied 3200 (to a Michelotti design) and the Ramseir Carrosserie of Worblaufen, Switzerland, also tried its skill on the 3.2 liter BMW chassis in 1960.

Ernst Loof produced the first prototype of the BMW 507, only to be edged out by the attractive Goertz design. Raymond Loewy built one custom body on the 507 chassis that still survives.

Karrosseriefabrik Karmann of Osnabrück, Germany, was responsible for coachwork on all the six-cylinder BMW coupes from the 2000C and CS models.

The East German Autovelo EMW and the British Bristol were discussed in earlier chapters. While none of these can be really considered true BMW's, their appearance at a gathering of BMW faithful would be welcomed—and they would be interesting cars, indeed, for collectors.

A few of these special BMW's are illustrated here. It's hard to value them for collector purposes, but suffice it to say their rarity and curiosity value would certainly be worth something.

At the Brussels Salon de L'Automobile in 1956, BMW showed a lovely Baur-bodied convertible 501A. Knock-off wheels were a bit incongruous with whitewall tires. Still, if you could find one of these today, you'd have quite a prize. (Courtesy Halwart Schrader)

Because they were blocky and bulbous, not many of these Ramseir two-doors were built on the 3.2 liter chassis in 1960. Ramseir built some Bristol bodies that were quite similar to this effort. A survivor would certainly cause a stir among BMW devotees. (Courtesy Halwart Schrader)

Trim Frua 2002 coupe was shown in Frankfurt in 1969. Italian curves just didn't match Munich's styling point of view at the time. Only one was built. (Courtesy Halwart Schrader)

Bristol of England built this 401 four-seater coupe from 1950-53. The two-liter BMW engine was modified extensively by the aircraft company. Aerodynamic Bristol was a sporty derivative of the BMW theme but its influence was not felt extensively in Germany. (BMW Werkphoto)

MODIFIED BMW'S

While BMW's have always been considered performance cars, some enthusiasts have had trouble leaving well enough alone. Although the hot-rodding phenomenon began in the US in the twenties, and special speed equipment for popular makes was manufactured, the emphasis for a long time was mainly on straight-line performance. In Germany, on the other hand, companies (called "tuners" originally) evolved from racing teams that capitalized on the unlimited autobahn speeds. Many of their special products were ordered for street cars whose abilities included high-speed handling.

It wasn't long before the top tuning firms, Alpina (Buchloe), Hartge (Beckingen) and Sohnitzer (Freilassing), began successfully applying lessons learned on the racetrack to a host of speed and handling equipment. In addition, these firms actually began creating their own cars by purchasing stripped BMW's from the factory and modifying them to suit a predetermined specification.

Customers could order, for example, an Alpina customized 5-Series car built to order. Or, individuals on a budget could select the components they wanted and tailor their own custom Bimmer.

A number of US firms act as agents for the German tuners. They import the special components and bring in complete, new, modified vehicles, certify them for the US and sell them in the currently legal "gray" market.

Interestingly, the BMW factory doesn't look askance at these hot-rodded cars. It developed close supporting relationships early on with the tuners when BMW's began to take an active role in racing. As well, as a BMW spokesman told me, "We like to watch the tuners as they sometimes experiment with ideas we feel aren't practical for most customers. Yet, if an idea seems popular, we'll incorporate it in our production cars." The 318i, with its air dam, spoiler, wide low-profile tires and redesigned suspension is a case in point.

The tuners, too, appreciate the cooperation they get from the factory. At Alpina, a spokesman told me they enjoyed a good relationship with the BMW engineers and ". . . sometimes they come down to Buchloe to see what we're doing and even to go for a fast ride."

If a modified BMW's your choice, the major tuners and their US agents, Hardy & Beck, Miller & Norburn, Performance Plus and others will happily assist you. If you want to modify your own BMW, or select the modifications and have them professionally installed, firms like Beaconwood Motors, Korman Autoworks, CTC and others will offer their services. And, if you want to import a European BMW, Teves Performance, European Auto Research, American Compliance and more than 100 other "gray marketers" are waiting to help.

There are a few caveats to any of these choices. You should ensure you have a source of spares and service, if you're not personally capable. Your BMW dealer will, as a rule, not be too hospitable to a European or heavily modified car. Also, be prepared to lose some money as you are unlikely to recoup the cost of the modifications easily. Many modified cars, however, appear for sale in the *Roundel* and *Autoweek*. If you know what you want, you can take advantage of the savings. Remember: Modified cars weren't bought to perk over to the 7-Eleven; they'll have been driven hard.

You can simply improve your car by upgrading springs and shocks, adding sway bars, halogen lights, special seats or a custom exhaust. These are relatively simple endeavors that, if done tastefully, can even add to a car's value. Extremes of any kind—a high-compression modified engine, removal of emission equipment, European bumpers, lowering, trick paint and so on—have just the reverse effect.

Personalizing your BMW, improving its performance, adding to its comfort and distinctiveness are other fun facets of these great vehicles. Be certain before you begin that you take all the advice here into consideration so you protect your investment.

The Germans call professional modifying "tuning." Alpina will build you a 2.8 liter 320 that will turn a seven-second 0-60 time and edge 140 mph. (Courtesy Alpina and Burkard Bovensiepen)

Heading for darkest Africa? This 320i is ready for low light and lots of bugs! (Author photo)

BMW Motorsport stripes and Sachs decals mark this German-styled modified car in the US. (Author photo)

Typical of German modified cars, this 3-Series was built by Wolfgang Marx, former director of the European BMW Car Clubs. Trim is painted body color, suspension modifications are evident. (BMWCCA *Roundel* photo courtesy Yale Rachlin)

BMW owners can't resist modifying their cars . . . here's an 02 with fender flares, lowered suspension, wide wheels and side exhaust. (Author photo)

The Hartge H5S. These cars were available in the US with a 3.5 liter 240 bhp engine for little more than the cost of a stock 533i. Suspension is stiff but with under 6.5-second 0-60 times with handling to match, who cares? For 1986 Performance Plus will take your stock 535i and update it to (even better) Hartge H5SP specs. (Courtesy Ivan C. Pato, Performance Plus, Inc.)

Autocross action: A close look at this 02 shows a roll bar, blacked-out trim and wide, modern rubber. (BMWCCA *Roundel* photo courtesy Yale Rachlin).

BMW CAR CLUBS

The BMW Car Club of America, Inc., is one of the largest (20,000 members) and best-organized car clubs. It publishes a very professional and informative monthly club magazine, the *Roundel*. The club has a number of regional groups and there are various specialized model sections for those people interested in particular BMW types such as the 2002tii or 507.

The BMWCCA's *Roundel* combines salon pieces on notable Bimmers with roadtests of new models, how-to's, restoration stories, owner testimonials and important "you heard it here first" factory information.

In addition, the *Roundel* classified section is an excellent source of enthusiast-maintained BMW's, often modified and improved by knowledgeable owners. These cars are frequently priced at a premium over Bimmers on dealers' lots or even other private sales. Often well-equipped, with a lot of goodies, they can often be bought at prices far less than the original cost of the add-ons.

The magazine is also crammed with advertising from all the BMW specialists, making it a terrific one-stop source each month for the latest in BMW accessories and performance parts.

In addition to regional meetings, the BMWCCA's annual Oktoberfest (held at a different location each year around the country) is a great opportunity for BMW aficionados to meet, look at each other's cars, attend a driving school, enter a rally or an autocross and prepare their cars to compete in a white-glove concours with knowledgeable BMW judges. For many Bimmerphiles, the Oktoberfest is a major event in their social calendars and they drive thousands of miles to attend.

Mark Luckman, the club's executive director, has a great deal of information available in his Cambridge, Massachusetts, office—as well as a supply of *Roundel* back issues and club regalia for sale. National dues are $17.50, $30 if you also join a local chapter. Write to the BMWCCA, Inc., 345 Harvard Street, Cambridge, MA 02138 (617) 492-2500.

Although the national club and BMW North America have no official connection, they are occasional combatants and reluctant allies. Mark Luckman feels it's important that the club remain objective and "... that's hard to do if you're being supported by the company itself." Frequently, the *Roundel* carries members' letters praising or criticizing BMW cars or the factory. And the club's roadtests are often quite critical. Basically the club's political drift is anti-eta and pro-performance. Many 02-Series owners regret they can't afford the 3-Series cars and this keeps the pages lively with comment and controversy. However, the membership also is a good source of constructive criticism, and with all these very interested repeat buyers as a captive audience, the factory and its American marketing organization pay close attention.

BMW Car Club of America
345 Harvard St.
Cambridge, MA 02138

BMW Vintage Club of America, Inc.
148 Linden St.
Wellesley, MA 02181

International Council of BMW Clubs
Peter Samuelson, President
Postfach 40 02 40
D-8000 München 40
West Germany

BMW Drivers Club of Australia
P.O. Box N45, Grosvenor St.
Sydney N.S.W. 2000, Australia

BMW Car Club of Canada
P.O. Box 232, Station "K," Toronto
Ontario, Canada M4P 2G5

The BMW Club Great Britain
Fred Secker
64 Calvary Drive
March, Cambs
PE 15 9EQ England

BMW Club Torino
Mario Borghesio
Via San Sanselmo 28
1-10125 Torino, Italy

Deutsch-Schweizer BMW Motorradclub
Felix Thoma
Zuricher Str. 241
CH-8953 Dietikon, Switzerland

323i Register
705 Main Street
Nocona, TX 76255

02 Series Touring
8731 W. 79th Avenue
Arvada, CO 80005

700
15931 Carrara Street
Hacienda Heights, CA 91745

3.0Si
5460 S.W. 65 Road
S. Miami, FL 33155

Isetta 300 and 600
Heinkel-Messerschmitt-Isetta Club
P.O. Box 90
Topanga, CA 90290

2000CS/CA 4 Cylinder Coupe
3498 Northwood Drive
Castro Valley, CA 94546

BMW Miniature Models
3210 East Maplewood
Littleton, CO 80121

BMW 507 Register
116 Grapevine Road
Wenham, MA 01984

1600GT
56-52 190th Street
Fresh Meadows, NY 11365

02 Series Cabriolet
17 Iroquoise Ave.
Allendale, NJ 07401

Senior Six Register
2500, 2800, Bavaria, 3.0S, etc.
3722 Randolph Road
Durham, NC 27705

2002tii
RD 1, Box 11
Almond, NY 14804

2002 Factory Turbo
4508 Littleton Place
La Canada, CA 91011

2800/3.0CS
4853 Cordell Ave #422
Bethesda, MD 20814

BMW Automobile Club of America
P.O. Box 401
Hollywood, CA 90078

PARTS AND SERVICE SOURCES

ALABAMA
Paeco Industries
213 South 21st St
Birmingham, AL 35233
205-323-8376
Performance parts and machine work

CALIFORNIA
XK-SS Inc
Box 4857
Thousand Oaks, CA 91359
213-991-1183
Replacement carpets, upholstery

Scheel California Inc
17101 S Central Ave, Unit 1
Carson, CA 90746
213-639-4570
Performance seats

AG Sales Group
PO Box 11027
Glendale, CA 91206
800-362-7380
213-790-2745
Performance accessories

JAM Engineering
PO Box 2750
244 Pearl St
Monterey, CA 93940
800-431-3533
408-372-1787
Weber carburetor conversions

Supersprint
3188 N Marks
Fresno, CA 93711
209-485-6451
Exhaust systems, mufflers

Reliable Motor Accessories
1751 Spruce St
Riverside, CA 92507
800-854-4770
714-781-0261
Accessories, car covers

National Auto Specialties
9471 Ridgehaven Ct
San Diego, CA 92123
800-854-2140
714-569-0202
Performance parts, accessories

Suspension Techniques
1853 Belcroft Ave
S. El Monte, CA 91733
213-442-7382
Performance parts

Primaflow Mufflers
1213 McDowell
Petaluma, CA 94952
800-732-3200
707-762-3002
Exhaust systems, mufflers

Automotive Performance Systems
620 S Flower St
Burbank, CA 91502
800-423-3623
213-841-3911
Performance parts and accessories

Beverly Hills Motoring Accessories
200 S Robertson Blvd
Beverly Hills, CA 90211
800-421-0911
213-657-4800
Accessories, car covers

Parts & Polish
12952 W Washington Blvd
Los Angeles, CA
213-391-8206
Performance parts, accessories

Far Horizon Auto Accessories
201 N Sullivan
Santa Ana, CA 92703
714-835-5533
Performance accessories, steering wheels

North Hollywood Speedometer & Clock Co
611 Lankersham Blvd
N. Hollywood, CA 91606
213-761-5136
VDO instrument service, speedometer conversions

Hardy & Beck
1799 Fourth St
Berkeley, CA 94710
415-526-5489
Performance parts, accessories

Prestige Motoring Accessories
18195 Euclid St
Fountain Valley, CA 92708
800-854-6770
714-966-2755
Accessories, car covers, tires

Triadco Enterprises
PO Box 1658
Turlock, CA 95381
209-668-0677
Dash covers and stereo protectors

European Racing Inc
2872 Walnut Ave
Tustin, CA 92680
714-838-7021
Wheels, performance accessories

Ieco
1431 Broadway
Santa Monica, CA 90404
213-451-1738
Performance parts, accessories

Bavarian Motor Parts
1424 S La Cienega Blvd
Los Angeles, CA 90035
213-652-4970
Service, parts, accessories

Bavarian Performance, Inc.
Dinau Engineering
81 Pioneer Way
Mountain View, CA 94041
415-962-9401
Suspension components

Ronal
15692 Computer Ln
Huntington Beach, CA 92649
714-891-4853
Modular wheels

Eurometrix
PO Box 1361
Campbell, CA 95008
Weber and Solex carburetor rebuilding

BAE
3032 Kashiwa St
Torrance, CA 90505
213-530-4743
Turbochargers

European Parts Specialists
828 Bond Ave
Santa Barbara, CA 93103
805-963-9696
OEM parts

German Motors Corp
1765 California (at Van Ness)
San Francisco, CA 94109
415-885-4060
Five-speed conversion kits

Pfaff Turbo
2152 O'Toole Ave
San Jose, CA 95131
408-946-9751
Single and twin turbo systems

Alpine Foreign Car Dismantlers
337 W Ave 26
Los Angeles, CA 90031
213-221-3126
Used BMW mechanical and body parts

Borla Industries
2639 Saddle Ave
Oxnard, CA 93030
805-983-7300
Stainless steel exhaust systems

CONNECTICUT
Callaway Turbo Systems
Stewarts Corner
Lyme, CT 06371
203-434-9002
Turbocharger systems

Performance Automotive
PO Box 10
Glastonbury, CT 06033
203-633-7868
Performance accessories

Kamei, Inc
300 Montowese Ave
North Haven, CT 06473
203-777-6676
Aerodynamic performance products

Panelcraft
3 Julius Dr
East Haven, CT 06513
203-467-2733
Sheetmetal parts

FLORIDA
Addco Industries Inc
906 Watertower Road
Lake Park, FL 33403
305-844-2531
Suspension components, sway bars

Performance Plus, Inc
1928 Tigertail Blvd
Bldg 12
Dania, FL 33004
305-922-9004
Service, parts, accessories, Hartge distributor

Meldeau Tire World
2270 N Semoran Blvd
Winter Park, FL 32792
305-678-3636
Tires, wheels

Coach Builders Ltd
Box 1978
High Springs, FL 32643
904-454-2060
Convertible conversions for 3- and 6-Series

GEORGIA
Alpharetta Auto Parts
5570 Hwy 19 N
Alpharetta, GA 30201
800-523-1929
Used parts

BJL Wholesale Auto Parts
PO Box 93805
Atlanta, GA 30318
404-351-5425
European and US spares

ILLINOIS
Midwest Auto Accessories & Parts
420 W 5th Ave
Naperville, IL 60540
800-323-5662
OEM and performance parts

INDIANA
E & F Electronics and Products
9159 Nora Ln
Indianapolis, IN 46240
317-283-1340
OEM and performance parts, stereos

IOWA
BBE International, Inc
310 East Prentiss
Iowa City, IA 52240
800-553-1234
319-351-9264
OEM parts, accessories

KENTUCKY
Louisville Lock & Key, Inc
317 Wallace Center #204D
Louisville, KY 40207
502-589-4127
Antitheft devices

MAINE
Datsun World
Auburn, ME 04210
207-784-4577
Service, parts, discount deliveries

MARYLAND/DC
Motorvation
PO Box 235
Brookeville, MD 20833
301-774-9442
Accessories

Autoy, Inc
4952 Wyaconda Rd
Rockville, MD 20852
301-468-4850
Performance suspension systems

Capital Cycle Corp
2328 Champlain St NW
Washington, DC 20009
202-387-7360
OEM parts, accessories

MASSACHUSETTS
Beaconwood Motors Inc
71 Rosedale Rd
Watertown, MA 02172
617-923-1050
Service, modifications, performance parts

Circle Tire Corp (CTC)
PO Box 175
Sherborn, MA 01770
617-655-7926
Service, OEM parts, accessories

European Auto Research
Rt 140
Upton, MA 01568
617-277-8954
European BMW's

Forte's Parts Connection
515 Moody St
Waltham, MA 02154
617-647-1530
OEM parts, accessories

Speedmark Ltd
123 N Beacon St
Boston, MA 02135
800-225-4380
617-254-4400
Parts, accessories, antitheft devices

Teves Performance
2 Falls St
Rehoboth, MA 02771
617-336-9050
European BMW's

Greenfield Imported Car Parts
409 Federal St
Greenfield, MA 01301
413-774-2819
Weber conversions

Jagco
37 Hiller Dr
Seekonk, MA 02771
320i stereo radio guards

Foreign Motors West
253 N Main St
Natick, MA 01760
617-653-4323
Spares for new and older BMW's

Black Forest Motors
1686 Commonwealth Ave
Boston, MA 02135
617-739-1145
Spares

MICHIGAN
Tricolor/Gobel of America
32330 W 12-Mile Rd
Farmington Hills, MI 48018
313-553-0155
Seat covers

MINNESOTA
Racing Unlimited, Inc
2607 Hennepin Ave S
Minneapolis, MN 55408
Race preparation, parts

MISSOURI
Imparts, Ltd
9330 Manchester Rd
St. Louis, MO 63119
800-325-9043
314-962-0810
Accessories, suspension kits

Mathis Marketing
4336 Rider Tr
Earth City, MO 63045
800-325-0610
314-291-2365
Wheels, tires

Metric Mechanic
2507 Truman Rd
Kansas City, MO 64127
816-483-5907
5-speeds for 02's

NEW JERSEY
Eurotire Inc
567 Rte 46
PO Box 1198
Fairfield, NJ 07006
800-631-1143
201-575-0080
Wheels, tires, installation

Kleban Suspension Systems
40 Railroad Ave
Hackensack, NJ 07601
201-488-3779
Bilstein shock absorbers

Johnson Automotive Engineering
23 Birch St
Midland Park, NJ 07432
201-652-3152
Service, parts, racing engines

DavMac
65 Brunswick Ave
Edison, NJ 08818
800-221-0738
201-287-4200
Wheels, tires, seats

Flemington BMW
Rte 202 & 31
Flemington, NJ 08822
201-782-9394
OEM BMW parts

JCM
198 Rt 206 S
Somerville, NJ 08876
201-359-2030
European tire chains

NEW HAMPSHIRE
Bavarian Auto Service, Inc
44 Exeter St
Newmarket, NH 03857
603-659-3282
Accessories, new and used parts

NEW YORK
EMAR International
123 E 54th St, Suite 6E
New York, NY 10022
212-486-6677
European BMW's

The Little Garage
69-14 48th Ave
Woodside, NY 11377
212-446-36¯0
Service, parts

Automat Co, Inc
225A Park Avenue
Hicksville, NY 11801
516-938-7373

Bavarian Auto Partz
Henry Noble
32 W 71st St 4A
New York, NY 10023
212-877-6807
New and used European parts

Conti Enterprise Corp
2023-119th St
College Point, NY 11356
212-358-1541
Ansa exhaust systems

Serra Autotecnica
1 Valhalla Pl
PO Box 78
Valhalla, NY 10595
914-681-0266
Performance parts, turbos

Motor Design
401 Jericho Tpke
New Hyde Park, NY 11040
800-648-6670
516-488-6670
Performance accessories

The A.A. P. Co
127-11 94th Ave
Richmond Hill, NY 11419
212-849-0800
Repco brake pads, Koni shocks

Bavarian Auto Parts
201-07 Northern Blvd
Bayside, NY 11361
718-423-5557 or 516-334-0322
European spares, performance parts

Zarkasky Enterprises
2 Daphne Ln
Centerport, NY 11721
516-757-8460
Spares, performance parts

NORTH CAROLINA
GMP
PO Box 240008
Charlotte, NC 28224
704-525-0941
Performance accessories, Zender distributor

Korman Autoworks
1316 Headquarters Dr
Greensboro, NC 27405
919-273-9604
Performance modifications, parts and accessories

Miller & Norburn, Inc
2002 E Peabody St
PO Box 11428
Durham, NC 27703
919-596-9309
Performance modifications, Alpina distributor

Karzundpartz
1B Wendy Court
PO Box 19289
Greensboro, NC 27419
800-334-2749
919-299-4646
Performance accessories

Bahnsport
1524 Battleground Ave
Greensboro, NC 27408
Performance accessories

American Compliance, Inc
PO Box 19272
Charlotte, NC 28219
704-525-0229
DOT/EPA certification for European BMW's

Hendrick Imports
6625 E Independence Blvd
Charlotte, NC 28212
704-535-0885
OEM parts, rebuilt engines

OHIO
MIAH
6660 Busch Blvd
Columbus, OH 43229
800-848-7383
614-885-5298
Parts, accessories

Racequip
809 Phillipi Rd
Columbus, OH 43228
614-276-5000
800-848-2973
Parts, accessories

Tabco
5250 Naiman Pkwy
PO Box 39474
Cleveland, OH 44139
216-248-5151
Body parts

OREGON

Quickor Engineering
6710 SW 111 Ave
Beaverton, OR 97005
505-645-9696
Performance parts, sway bars

V. Polak
2239 NW Raleigh St
Portland, OR 97210
800-547-1788
503-295-0733
Steering wheels, accessories

PENNSYLVANIA

Two Thousand Two Products Inc
503 Monroe Dr
Harleysville, PA 19438
215-362-7757
OEM parts, accessories

Air Automotive
1211 Hanover Ave
Allentown, PA 18103
215-437-2722
Remanufactured BMW's

Zygmunt Motors
70 Green St
Doylestown, PA 18901
215-348-3121
Parts and accessories

Headercraft Inc
PO Box 2322
York, PA 17405
717-845-6100
Exhaust headers

Stahl Headers
1515 Mt Rose Ave
York, PA 17403
717-846-1632
Exhaust headers

Subtle Dynamics
5119 West Chester Pike
Newtown Square, PA 19073
215-356-9600
Performance accessories

Bimmer Parts Co
Box 672
Pottstown, PA 19464
215-326-3502
OEM parts, accessories

SOUTH CAROLINA

Bavarian Motor Cars
Greenville, SC 29602
803-288-0158
Service and parts

TENNESSEE

Richard Bayston Automotive Innovations
PO Box 80361
Chattanooga, TN 37411
615-629-2640
Antishimmy kits

TEXAS

German Partshaus
1701 N Greenville Ave
Richardson, TX 75081
214-783-1720
OEM performance parts, accessories

Nine-Eleven Enterprises, Inc
2750 Northaven, Suite 207
Dallas, TX 75229
800-527-5632
214-241-2002
Performance accessories, books

Phoenix Motor Works
1508 Fortview
Austin, TX 78704
512-442-1361
Parts, service

Euro-Import, Inc
1167 Britmoore Rd
Houston, TX 77043
713-465-7756
Fender trim sets

Bavarian Motor Sports
1812 Reliance Pkwy, Suite A
Bedford, TX 76021
1-800-Alpina-1
817-BMS8215
Alpina performace components

VERMONT

Mountain Auto Sport
Rte 141
Proctersville, VT 05153
802-226-7781
Performance tuning, fabrication

VIRGINIA

Electrodyne
2316 Jefferson Davis Hwy
Alexandria, VA 22313
800-336-3096
Parts, accessories

International Auto Systems
1309 Mountain View St
Charlottesville, VA 22901
804-295-0128
Exhaust systems

WASHINGTON

Alan BMW Saab
2140 Hwy 99
Edmonds, WA 98020
206-771-7100
OEM parts, accessories

WEST VIRGINIA

BSR-Schrick
PO Box 190
Summit Point, WV 25446
304-725-5270
High-performance camshafts

Tire America
One Bryan Dr
Wheeling, WV 26003
800-624-6932
Wheels, tires

WISCONSIN

Classic Motorbooks
P.O. Box 2
Osceola, WI 54020
800-826-6600
715-294-3345
Literature and manuals